T0165839

Praise for
God of Becoming and Relationship:
The Dynamic Nature of Process Theology

"Through honesty, openness and erudition, Rabbi Artson teaches of a God who whispers 'grow' to each of us. A beautiful and soulful exploration."

—**Rabbi David Wolpe**, Sinai Temple, Los Angeles, California;
author, *Why Faith Matters*

"Offers us a new way to see ourselves, our world and our God. We no longer have to choose between our faith and our intellect. What a joy and what a relief it is to be able to integrate these seeming disparities. This important work invites us into a relationship with a God who is dynamic and loving. This is a book that can heal our souls."

—**Rabbi Naomi Levy**, spiritual leader, Nashuva;
author, *Hope Will Find You, Talking to God,* and *To Begin Again*

"Shows how Process Theology can give us the language and understanding to forge a moral and compelling Judaism for ourselves.... If you have wrestled with the presence of evil in the world and suffering in your private life—if you have struggled to find a belief in God that is scientifically tenable and an approach to Torah that is intellectually credible—then this book is for you. It will inspire and nurture your soul."

—**Rabbi Irving "Yitz" Greenberg**, founding president,
the Jewish Life Network; author, *The Jewish Way*

"I wept for joy reading this book. So many of us are wounded by conventional vocabulary when we think and talk about God—our language is stuck, and we are stuck. Artson, one of the most inspiring Jewish leaders and theologians of our time, redeems the ancient covenant of formulating anew our conversation about God."

—**Rabbi Tamar Elad-Appelbaum**, founding rabbi,
Zion: An Eretz Israeli community in Jerusalem

"The truth of the matter is: After reading this book you will want to become Jewish, if you aren't already. Or, to be more exact, a Jew with a Process perspective. The insights from this book come so naturally and flow so freely from its pages, weaving together Jewish wisdom and Process philosophy, that you are drawn to a way of living that is deeply loving, deeply traditional, deeply creative and deeply faithful, without leaving your mind at the door or your heart on a shelf.... I plan to use this book again and again in the classroom, sharing it with people of many faiths and no faith.... An exciting achievement."

—**Jay McDaniel, PhD**, author, *Of God and Pelicans: Theology of Reverence for Life* and *Living from the Center: Spirituality in an Age of Consumerism*; editor, Jesus, Jazz, and Buddhism (www.jesusjazzbuddhism.org)

"A pioneering exploration of collaborative ecumenical thinking. Illustrates the complementary and contrasting features in Judaism and Process Theology. In broadening the horizons of the search for wholeness, Artson opens a fantastic adventure of ideas."

—**Rabbi Harold M. Schulweis**, author, *Conscience: The Duty to Obey and the Duty to Disobey*; founder, Jewish Foundation of the Righteous and the Jewish World Watch

"Extraordinary ... speaks to the real-world experience of many people who find a fixed set of religious beliefs and teachings incompatible with what they know.... Explicates a twenty-first-century Judaism that is dynamic, constructive, ethical and deeply meaningful; offers ways for us to think about prayer, ritual and Israel, and about what we must do to create greater justice."

—**Ruth W. Messinger**, president, American Jewish World Service

"With personal, persuasive prose ... skillfully presents a theology to live with and live by. It may change the way that you think about God, Judaism and your being in the world."

—**Sue Levi Elwell, PhD**, rabbinic director, East Geographic Congregational Network Union for Reform Judaism

"Undertakes the daunting challenge of spelling out a theology that will speak to the mind and soul of the modern reader, and succeeds."

—**Rabbi Harold Kushner**, author, *When Bad Things Happen to Good People*

"An amazing combination of personal narrative, introduction to Process Thought and integration of Jewish theology with the two. It should open up to a whole new community the fruitfulness of thinking about God, life and Judaism through Process perspectives."

—**Thomas Jay Oord**, author, *The Nature of Love* and *Defining Love*

"Both a lovely, poetic introduction to Process Theology, and a vivid sense of Rabbi Artson's private journey as a believer, a Jewish leader, a father, a teacher and a Jew.... His enthusiasm and compassion are on every page, inviting you to learn from him and with him."

—**Laurie Zoloth**, director, Center for Bioethics, Science and Society, Northwestern University

"Brings to pass a confluence of Process Theology and Judaism hitherto only hinted at. The vibrant Jewishness of his sources, practices and rhythms of interpretation yield an unsurpassed introduction to the God of becoming—for all children of Sarah, Hagar, Abraham."

—**Catherine Keller**, professor, theology, Drew University; author, *On the Mystery: Discerning Divinity in Process.*

"The most comprehensive exposition of a Jewish Process Theology yet written. Jews and Gentiles alike are indebted to Rabbi Artson for the intellectual-theological-emotional achievement this book represents."

—**Rabbi David Ellenson**, president, Hebrew Union College– Jewish Institute of Religion

"[A] work of honest struggle by a fellow-seeker for a believable Jewish theology in our day.... Don't miss it!"

—**Arthur Green**, rector, Rabbinical School, Hebrew College

"With sensitivity, wit and profundity, Rabbi Artson makes it possible for those who long ago abandoned the jealous-coercive-angry-old-man God to forge a new path to spiritual depth and holiness…. Simply said, with this book, [he] gives us God back."

—**Rabbi Sharon Brous**, founding rabbi, IKAR

"Until now it has been chiefly Protestants who have profited from the brilliant work of Alfred North Whitehead in reformulating ideas about God, the world and our inner lives. Now, in using Whitehead to revitalize Jewish life and thought, Brad Artson outdoes and inspires us all."

—**John B. Cobb Jr.**, professor emeritus, Claremont School of Theology

"If you own only one book on Jewish Process Theology, this should be [it]. Accessible, persuasive and richly rooted in Jewish texts, Artson's theology is warm and inviting where Mordecai Kaplan's is cold and distant."

—**Rachel Adler**, David Ellenson Professor of
Modern Jewish Thought, Hebrew Union College

"Wide ranging and pensive…. Pioneering…. Anyone reading this enthusiastic vision of Judaism will be swept along by the author's enthusiasm."

—*Spirituality & Practice*

GOD
of Becoming
and
Relationship

Other Jewish Lights Books
by Rabbi Bradley Shavit Artson, DHL

Passing Life's Tests:
Spiritual Reflections on the Trial of Abraham, the Binding of Isaac

Renewing the Process of Creation:
A Jewish Integration of Science and Spirit

GOD
of Becoming *and* Relationship

THE DYNAMIC NATURE
OF PROCESS THEOLOGY

Rabbi Bradley Shavit Artson, DHL

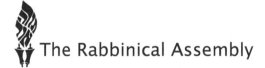

The Rabbinical Assembly

For People of All Faiths, All Backgrounds

JEWISH LIGHTS Publishing

Nashville, Tennessee

God of Becoming and Relationship:
The Dynamic Nature of Process Theology

2016 Quality Paperback Edition, First Printing

Essays in this volume are reprinted with permission from *Conservative Judaism* © Rabbinical Assembly (Vol. 62, #1–2, Fall/Winter 2010–2011).

© 2013 by Bradley Shavit Artson

Library of Congress Cataloging-in-Publication Data
Artson, Bradley Shavit.
  God of becoming and relationship : the dynamic nature of process
  theology / Rabbi Bradley Shavit Artson, DHL.
    pages cm
"For people of all faiths, all backgrounds."
Includes bibliographical references.
ISBN 978-1-58023-713-0
1. God (Judaism) 2. Judaism and science. 3. Process Theology. I. Title.
BM610.A798 2013
296.3—dc23
                                    2013031981
ISBN 978-1-58023-876-2 (pbk)
ISBN 978-1-58023-788-8 (eBook)

10 9 8 7 6 5 4 3 2 1

Manufactured in the United States of America
Cover Design: Heather Pelham
Cover Art: © istockphoto.com/pdiaz
Interior Design: Kelley Barton

For People of All Faiths, All Backgrounds
Published by Jewish Lights Publishing
An imprint of Turner Publishing Company
Nashville, Tennessee
Tel: (615) 255-2665   Fax: (615) 255-5081
www.jewishlights.com
www.turnerpublishing.com

For Elana

Contents

Introduction

I live in west Los Angeles in a home that was built in the 1950s. Our dining room has wood paneling along its four walls. When we first bought the house a decade ago, the room was painted a sickly green, presumably in the late '70s during the high-water mark of the aesthetics of *The Brady Bunch* and *The Partridge Family*. The actual wood grain and tone were covered; I think in that era people thought such a look was cutting-edge. With that greenish coat of paint, the walls looked fake and cheap. When we finally got around to repainting the upstairs of the house, we asked our painter if he could just coat the paneling a simple white because the green was hideous. He pondered for a moment, then took his thumbnail and scratched on the paneling. The paint peeled away, and he said, "You know, I think that under this green there is actual wood." His team spent three days sandblasting and varnishing. At the end of the week our dining room was transformed! The wood appears rich and the patterns in the grain are magnificent; it is now my favorite room in the house. I had thought, erroneously, that the wall itself was that sickly green when, in fact, that trashy look was just the coating that someone had painted over the shimmering wood.

Modern Westerners often approach religion as I did the paneling: they assume that the only way to be religious is to accept the sickly green overlay of Greek philosophy. They take neo-platonized Aristotelian scholastic presuppositions and filter religion through those ideas. Then, because they have insurmountable problems with those assertions, they assume that the quandary involves religion itself, or the Bible, or the Talmud, or observance, or God. What Process Theology offers is the opportunity to sandblast the philosophical overlay of Hellenistic Greece and medieval Europe off the rich, burnished grain of Bible, Rabbinics, and Kabbalah so that we can savor the actual patterns in the living wood of religion, the *etz hayyim*,[1] and appreciate Judaism for what it was intended to be and truly is.

Much like what the sandblasting did for our perspective on our dining room, this book offers the tools to relate to the world anew: not as the bumping together of solid substances in absolute space and time, but as a world of shimmering particles of energy that interact constantly and eternally. Every creature is a resilient pattern of interlocking energy, each in a developing process of becoming. Because *becoming* is concrete and real, and *being* is only a logical abstraction, the distillation of becoming in pure thought, Process Thought focuses on becoming as the central mode of every creature, of all creation, and indeed of the Creator as well. The universe is recognized as a series of interacting, recurrent energy patterns, but not one that endlessly loops in the same repetitive patterns. Instead, the surprising miracle of our universe is that it seems to generate novelty with each new moment of continuing creation. New stars, new galaxies, and new elements combine and create new possibilities. At least once, a galaxy with sufficient stability and diversity produced at least one solar system with at least one planet on which the slow and gradual evolution of self-conscious life could—and did—emerge.

In such a worldview, God is not outside the system as some unchanging, eternal abstraction. Rather, God permeates every aspect of becoming, indeed grounds all becoming by inviting us and every level of reality to fulfill our own optimal possibilities. The future remains open, through God's lure, to our own decisions of how or what we will choose next. God, then, uses a persistent, persuasive power, working in each of us (and all creation at every level) to nudge us toward the best possible outcome. But God's power is not coercive and not all-powerful. God cannot break the rules or unilaterally dictate our choices. Having created and then partnered with this particular cosmos, God is vulnerable to the choices that each of us makes freely as co-creators.

An Overview of Process Thought

What I've set out to do is introduce you to Process Thought (focusing for our purposes on Process Theology) and Process Philosophy, a wonderful systematic approach to making sense of the world—not just of one aspect of it, but the world as a whole—and the ethical implications that living in dynamic relationship reveal. Process Thought, a speculative system, looks at the underlying postulates that make the world what it is and describes how all its components relate in a dynamic and participatory unfolding. Process Theology uses Process Thought as a powerful tool for integrating religion and science in a way that respects the integrity of both disciplines as valid ways to relate to the world and to each other. Process Theology also provides an insightful hermeneutical tool to explicate the layers of meaning of ancient scripture (particularly the Bible and, in this book, Rabbinics). This methodology comprises a constellation of ideas sharing the common assertions that:

- The world and God are expressions of continuous, dynamic relational change. We label that process as creativity. The mutual commitment to that process is faithfulness (*emunah*), which rises above any faith (doctrine or creed).

- We and the world are not solid substances, but rather recurrent patterns of energy, occasions that change with each new instantiation but also maintain continuity from moment to moment.

- We are interconnected, each to each and each to all. Therefore all creation—not just humanity or a subset of humanity—has value and dignity.

- Every occasion has an interiority (first person mode, subjective) appropriate to its nature as well as an outer (third person, objective) way of related interaction and becoming. That is, we are all selves-in-relation.

- We and every occasion relate to each and all creation instantaneously and intuitively. We respond to the decisions of each other and of the totality, as we ourselves are re-created in each instant.

- God is the One who makes this relating possible, who creates the openness of a future of real novelty and the variety of its possibilities, and who relates to each of us in our particular individuality.

- God is the One who invites us—and empowers us—in our particularity (hence, God knows us and relates to us as individuals) to select the optimal choice for our own flourishing (optimal in terms of maximizing experience, justice, compassion, and love) and for our mutual flourishing. To exist is to be self-determining, interconnected, and creative to some degree.

- We and everything in the cosmos become co-creators with God in fashioning the present (which has primacy) out of the possibilities offered by the future and the constraints imposed by the past. God's primary mode of power is persuasive, not coercive. That goes for us, too.

- Once the present becomes actual, it is known eternally by God and cherished forever.

These convictions may seem unsettling at first glance, but I will try to show that they actually reflect what you already know to be true about yourself, all life, and the cosmos. We take for granted what it means to be conventionally religious, and then struggle to reconcile our beliefs with the kind of lives we seek to live, because those traditionalist assumptions often make it difficult to open ourselves in an engaging and explanatory way to articulate what we intuit and to connect to each other, the world, and the Divine with an embracing faithfulness.

To enable us to better embrace that faithfulness, I want to flag two distinctive translations that are offered to help open the sources for us: while I generally follow the new Jewish Publication Society translation of the Hebrew Bible, I do not mistranslate the Tetragrammaton (God's four-letter name *Y-H-W-H*) as "Almighty" or "Sovereign." Those translations, although widespread, are both inaccurate and misleading, conscripting an archaic title of feudal status instead of conveying the flowing temporal nature of God's holy becoming *and* the timeless quality of God's essence. To try to capture the numinous ineffability of the Name, I generally translate it as the "One" or the "Holy One." There is no way to really translate the Name, let alone to verbalize it. We can only breathe God's Name. Similarly, you may be used to seeing *Ha-kadosh Baruch Hu* translated as the "Holy One, blessed be He." But God is the ground of all blessing, transcending all gender, and a better translation would be "Holy Bountiful One" or "Holy Blessing One,"[2] which is how you will find it translated in this book. I hope that these fresh translations will help you break through to a fresh relationship with the One who exceeds all verbal description and through whom all possibilities emerge.

Our Two-Tiered Exploration

Process Thought's relational way of describing the cosmos and the Divine, the nature of becoming and of reality, changes our understanding of creation, revelation, commandments, ethics, prayer, Israel, death, freedom, and love. Accordingly, this book offers a two-tiered opportunity to grow in this new understanding.

Part 1 offers an introduction to the main concepts of Process Thought, Process Theology, and Process Philosophy, in part, by comparing major Process themes, particularly those that pertain to religion and spirituality—God, creation, relationships, revelation, death—with dominant Western theologies. I draw from my own experience, the work of Process theologians and philosophers, as well as biblical and rabbinic sources.

As mentioned above, Process Theology may seem new and unsettling at first, but in part 2, I aim to quell any remaining disquiet by showing that significant strands within Judaism have always been inherently Process. I look at some major aspects of Judaism—the Jewish relationship with God; the Jewish understanding and commitment to covenant; rituals and observances, including prayer, *mitzvot*, and holy days; the Jewish relationship to Israel; our understanding of mortality and meaning; the importance of community and the pursuit of justice—and illustrate a way of life, a cultural and spiritual expression, that from its very roots is dynamic, interconnected, and in continuous relational change.

In both parts, a dual agenda pulsates: applying the key insights of Process Theology to the topic at hand, and mobilizing Jewish sources to demonstrate what a powerful hermeneutical tool Process Thought can be for unlocking the true power and resonance of Jewish sources and wisdom. Because a Process approach modifies or transcends many assumptions about religion and about the reality of the world, this book will not follow the conventional path of a linear argument. Instead of starting with an axiom and then deploying reason coercively to force consent to a single conclusion, this book will follow a process of contemplative meandering, as we circle a growing intimacy, swirl with an understanding that undulates and swings from one thought to another. Processing along this labyrinth, this circle of growing recognition, entails some repetition and revisiting and a good deal of mindfulness. Walking a pilgrim's labyrinth is how we advance with our feet and unify heart, mind, and soul. A Process exploration should involve nothing less.

I conclude the book on a personal note, first with my affirmation of Judaism that models a pervasive Process perspective and by sharing the balm of Process Thought to my son Jacob's struggle with autism.

For readers who find philosophy difficult or for those with no prior exposure to Process Thought, let me suggest you begin at the end: with the letter to my son and my personal affirmation of Judaism. Those selections will allow you to feel Process Thought from the inside. Then, armed with these new intuitions, you can begin again at the beginning, now with a compass that can direct your reading more productively.

Who Should Read This Book?

I wrote this book for you if you want to be able to locate your life in a single, encompassing story, one that includes everything from the first moment the universe began until yesterday, a narrative that embraces deepest personal meaning, a yearning to love and be loved, a quest for social justice and compassion. I wrote this book for you if you feel wounded by conventional religion, with its domineering God and not infrequent assaults on common sense, scientific method, and human dignity, or if you feel wounded by combative secularism and its not infrequent assaults on any real sense of purpose, transcendence, or belonging. I wrote this book for Jews who are seeking a way to integrate their admiration for Jewish values and ethics with a spirituality that cannot put on blinders and forget what their minds learned in science labs and history classes. I also wrote this book for non-Jews who are interested in what wisdom Judaism might contribute to their lives but cannot endure yet another system of counterintuitive faith and mandated obedience. And I wrote this book for all of us, beyond labels, seeking a way to celebrate the dynamism and unity of this marvelous, mysterious, awe-filled world. Finally, I wrote this book for myself, so I could continue to hold onto Torah as a way of life without abandoning or betraying my best values and the people I love most.

How Is This Book Different?

While there are several superb presentations of Process Thought already available, this one is unique in at least one way: it doesn't assume a normative Protestant perspective as its home base.

First articulated by philosopher and mathematician Alfred North Whitehead (1861–1947), Process is a way of accounting for the cosmos as a dynamic, evolving unity (including relativity theory and quantum mechanics) and was meant to provide a philosophical, speculative system accessible to all. His primary advocates in succeeding generations were extraordinary Protestant theologians and their students. As a result, most presentations of Process Thought rely on Christian religion and institutions and wrestle with specifically Christian issues—the status of the Trinity, the nature of Jesus. Understandably central for Christians exploring how they could better express their faith through a Process lens, this focus lends an unintended parochial constraint if it is the only way that Process Theology is approached. As a rabbi and a theological philosopher, I am interested in contributing to a vibrant community of diverse faiths (and secularities) that can each use Process insights as a way to build communities that are robust in their pluralism *and* rooted in their streams of wisdom. While my examples and illustrations are derived primarily from Jewish tradition and scripture, I share with my non-Jewish Process colleagues a deep joy in bringing people and traditions together without erasing their distinctiveness. All are welcome here.

My Personal Discovery

Like many others who have found a home in Process Thought, I was first motivated by a combination of ethical outrage—in my case, the struggles of my son, Jacob, with his autism—and the double betrayal of conventional religion (his autism is for the good, is a mystery, must have been the result of some previous sin, is meant to teach a lesson) and material secularism (there is no purpose, we are all doomed in a universe of complete indifference, Jacob doesn't measure up by worldly standards, he's not a good investment). I was looking for a deeper explanation that could restore hope, strengthen our resolve to work to lift Jacob's burden, and open to him a life of joy and meaning. Still, I needed to remain open to what I knew about reality from my study of science and history. This drove me to articulate a different sense of reality: one of dynamic becoming, interactive relating, and a cosmos free to participate in shaping an open future of meaning. Imagine my delight and surprise to discover that Process Theology had already been created a century earlier! Rooted in the remarkable insights of Henri Bergson, William James, John Dewey, Charles Sanders Pierce and the American Pragmatists, and others, this approach received its most explicit and detailed presentation in Whitehead's brilliant, comprehensive writings. He developed his insights as a professor of philosophy at Harvard University, and his work was advanced by several students. Some continued to explicate Process implications for philosophical speculation as a whole, and some focused on its implications for theology and religion, most notably scholars like Charles Hartshorne of the University of Chicago. Hartshorne, in turn, was blessed by extraordinary students, foremost among them John Cobb and David Ray Griffin, both of the Claremont School of Theology. At present, Process Philosophy enjoys many advocates, and Process Theology is often described as one of, if not the most energetic and influential of American expressions of theology.

A second and equally surprising discovery was the realization that while most Jews were unaware of Process Theology, there have been several prominent Jewish thinkers who consider their work somehow related to its cluster of insights, among them Mordecai Kaplan, Max Kadushin, Milton Steinberg, and, to some degree, Abraham Joshua Heschel, Harold Kushner, Harold Schulweis, and Arthur Green. While there are real distinctions between Kaplanian Reconstructionism and Whiteheadian Process, there are enough similarities and shared ethics (not to mention footnote citations) to recognize the salutary influence of Process insights and to suggest that many Jews (and non-Jews) would welcome an accessible, explicit presentation of Process Theology.

This volume represents the harvest of a lifetime's quest. Raised in a secular home that treasured learning, personal integrity, human dignity, and social justice, I learned firsthand to resist parroting other people's convictions if I did not share them and to dissociate myself from ideas that marginalized or denigrated others. Those childhood values remain my core. In college, I fell in love with God for the first time and found my way to a traditional and egalitarian version of

Jewish faithfulness at Harvard Hillel. In that journey I found the extraordinary woman who is, to this day, my best friend and wife (and to whom this book is gratefully dedicated). Her Israeli family opened up to me a sense of peoplehood and Hebrew culture that enhanced my journey. At some point, when I was disillusioned with the world of professional politics—although still passionate about justice, dignity, inclusion, and our planet—Elana suggested that I train for the rabbinate. That period gave me a vocabulary, access to the rich streams of Jewish scriptures (biblical, rabbinic, philosophical, and mystical), and deepened my religious practice. I emerged as the rabbi of a growing young congregation in California, where I started putting my ideas to the test of real life. With the birth of our twins, Jacob and Shira, the real journey began anew. Jacob's diagnosis of autism shook every conviction and made clear that my conventional liberal theology was a paste job, inadequate to the task at hand: fighting so my son could live a life of joy and significance. After ten years as a congregational rabbi, I found my way to Los Angeles and American Jewish University (then the University of Judaism) as dean of its Ziegler School of Rabbinic Studies. Together with its hardy band of extraordinary scholars, rabbis, and students, I renewed my own quest for an integrated understanding of the world and my life that would grant me renewed purpose, strength, and uplift. I enrolled in a doctoral program, under the sage and kind Rabbi Dr. David Ellenson of Hebrew Union College–Jewish Institute of Religion, as the structure I would need to find the treasure I sought, and Process Theology is the treasure I uncovered. My wife tells me that I pursued a doctorate instead of therapy—and I think she's right! My own interlocking Jewish communities (Conservative/Masorti Judaism here and worldwide; IKAR; the faculty, administration, and students of American Jewish University; my rabbinic and Jewish colleagues across the spectrum of practice and ideology), augmented by the welcoming and generous scholars and advocates of Process Theology, have given me back my life, renewed my hope, and restored my sense of belonging.

Dissolving the Fallacy of the Dichotomy

If this is your first encounter with Process Thought, much of what this book has to offer may initially sound shocking, perhaps even irreligious. This is because much of what we were told we *should* believe about God, about the physical universe, about our consciousness when we were younger (or even by many religious leaders today) forces us to choose between our spirit and our intellect, between science and religion, between morality and dogma. In such a split, most decent human beings would, with reluctance, choose intellect, science, and morality.

But here's the precious gift of Process Thought: this dichotomy, this choice of either A or B, is a false bifurcation. We can understand the world, God, and religion in such a way that we don't have to make that choice at all. Indeed, armed with Process insights and tools, we can affirm that our religiosity, our spirit, our minds, and our ethics all strengthen and refine each other.

As you persist, you may discover, as many others have, that you need not put up a wall between what you know and what you believe, that science and religion need not remain locked in a winner-take-all battle, that there is a way to embrace the poetry and wisdom of ancient faiths without having to adopt morally or intellectually compromised positions, that you can be religious without checking your education or morality at the door.

If you are seeking such a path, then this book is my offering to you. I hope you find its insights and possibilities liberating and alluring. I hope you are able to use these Process ideas and examples to sandblast away your own oppressive patinas, your own false slick surfaces. I invite you to rediscover the rich, moist wood at your core: alive, rooted, and growing toward the sun. We are, each of us, living trees, and together we constitute a forest ancient and resurgent, populated with many different and verdant kinds, each of us joining together to create an arbor for life, for diversity, and for ever more intimate relationships of justice and love.

Part I

On the Way
An Introduction
to Process Theology

Part 1 of this book explains Process Thought, a systematic approach to the world, to life, and to humanity that seeks to integrate what we know and what we feel into a single, united narrative of dynamic interrelationship and becoming. Building upon the insight that the world is dynamic and interrelated, Process Thought articulates that every creature exists in relationship to each other and to all creation, and that everything is always becoming and self-determining within the parameters of what has gone before and what is being determined by the rest of existence.

Process Thought is first and foremost a response to the challenge posed by the dynamic and interrelated nature of reality: making sense of what exists, given our knowledge of relativity theory, quantum physics, cosmology, evolutionary biology, cognitive science and neurology, psychology, history, religion, and literature. Within Process Philosophy, a bold group of daring clergy and philosophical theologians applied these insights to the questions raised by religion, and in Process Theology they advanced tremendous possibilities for a faithfulness that is honest, open, spiritually rich, and ethically engaged in the world.

Part 1 will present the building blocks of this Process understanding of the world. Our focus will be on the teachings and

1

insights of Process Thought, with our primary examples and illustrations derived from Hebrew scriptures, rabbinic literature, and Jewish philosophy. Still, our central attention will be on the core questions that animate all Process Philosophy.

Chapter 1 explores what it means to recognize God as dynamic and vulnerable, as using persuasive power to enlist us to make optimal choices for our own (and creation's) betterment. If God is dynamic and persuasive, then, as we will see in chapter 2, our narrative of creation will adapt accordingly, both to accommodate our scientific knowledge of the cosmos and of life and to accommodate our own sense of freedom and partnership.

Chapter 3 takes the dynamic God into relationship with the dynamic cosmos and illumines the biblical notion of covenant. In that discussion, the centrality of both choice and love will become clear. The significance of love also becomes clear in chapter 4's exploration of creation not as a single event in the past, but as a continuous process engaging God and the world in ever new expression.

Love must become manifest as justice. Any honest look at the world as it is must come to terms with the suffering of innocents and the prevalence of evil. Chapter 5 uses a Process perspective and the teachings of Maimonides to shift our struggle with evil from an intellectual exercise to a call to action to alleviate suffering.

With chapter 6, we will explore the ways that this dynamic integration shifts and deepens our sense of revelation—the many levels at which God communicates with creation and the unique ways that humans both receive and shape that communication. Process gives us vital tools to appreciate the Bible's spiritual and cognitive components and how God and humanity "converse" on primal and verbal levels.

Finally, in chapter 7, we will address the mystery of all mysteries: our mortality and the meaning of death, illumined by the distinctive thinking that Process makes possible.

1

The Living, Luring God
Recovering a Biblically
and Rabbinically Rooted Divine

*Any exploration of theology should begin with an articulation of our under-*standing of God—what God is, what God isn't, and what God can be. In Western culture, we are habituated to ancient Greek and medieval European ways of religious thinking. As a result, we assume that is what religion necessarily entails: specifically, the kind of theology that most Christian theologians call "classical." By this they mean Augustine, Aquinas, and the broad spectrum of medieval philosophy, which presupposes that God must be simple and eternal, unchanging, and therefore omnipotent, omniscient, and omnibenevolent.[1] Based on these presumptions, God has—and must have—all the power. That is what *omnipotent* means.[2] God has—and must have—all knowledge, knowing everything that is, was, and will be. God is omnibenevolent—pure good. The challenge for many of us is that certain intolerable consequences spring from these three axioms. Process Theology helps us understand God in a way that circumvents this quandary.

The Good, the Bad, and the Powerful

Let's begin with a close look at an all-powerful God and the problems this view creates. For God to be omnipotent implies that no power exists that is not God's, which means, first of all, that

anything that happens is God's responsibility. Sometimes we like
what happens, sometimes we do not. Regardless, everything that
happens comes from God. So God gets the credit for anything good
in life; for anything bad in life, God gets the blame. There is no
escape from that inexorable logic, which engenders many people's
vehement rejection of religion. A God who could have stopped "X"
but did not is a God most of us want nothing to do with. Everyone,
at some point in life, suffers terrible trauma. At the moments that
monotheists most need God and a sense of God's love, they are
coerced by their Greek-influenced theology into conceding that God
must have had a legitimate reason to cause (or at least to not prevent) the trauma from occurring. The fault, by default, must be their
own. That relentless conclusion leads them to do what far too many
Western people have done across the millennia, which is to abandon their moral compass and generally reliable sense of right and
wrong in order to blame themselves or their loved ones when bad
things happen.[3] The inescapable consequence of this theological
straitjacket is that not only does something horrible happen, but the
victims, already burdened by their suffering, also feel delinquent,
abandoned, or punished.

But there is yet another way in which the concept of omnipotence creates an insurmountable challenge. Power is always relational. One has power only to the extent that one has more of it than
someone else does. To the extent that one has *all* the power, one
actually has no power whatsoever, because power only works when
there are two parties engaged in a power dynamic, one the object of
the power of the other. Without that relationship, there is no possibility of demonstrating or using power at all. Absolute power is self-
erasing.[4] The philosophical presumption that God is omnipotent
has been reinforced by the fact that many translations of the Bible
refer to God as the "Almighty," which derives from a mistranslation
of *El Shaddai*.[5] The Torah has terms for great power and unsearch-
able strength—"Great is the Holy One, and much acclaimed" (Psalm
145:3) and "the One who performs great deeds which cannot be

fathomed" (Job 9:10)—but it has neither the concept nor a term for omnipotence. The prophets have no such label; neither does the Talmud. There is no classical Hebrew or Aramaic term for being able to do absolutely everything. In fact, that medieval philosophical concept leads to clever theological tricks. For example, a person is more powerful than God because it is possible for a person to construct a weight so heavy that she cannot lift it. If God is all-powerful, then God too should be able to create a weight so powerful that God cannot lift it. But if God cannot lift it, or if God cannot make such a weight, then God is not all-powerful. That kind of conundrum of language highlights the fact that this particular concept of omnipotence is fatally flawed.

The Bible and the Rabbis portray God as vastly, persistently powerful, but not as all-powerful.

Know Everything, No Freedom

A similar conflict emerges with the claim that God is all-knowing. Omniscience assumes that God knows everything, including the future as well as the past. Nothing is hidden from an all-knowing God. But if God knows the future absolutely, then there is no room for divine or creaturely freedom. Human beings know the future probabilistically: I know that it is likely that if I write in an interesting way, you will be able to focus most of the time on the words you are now reading. That is probably true, and I have written and read enough that I can reasonably expect that what has been true in the past will most likely continue to be true in the future. But I do not know absolutely. Today something could have happened in your life to make it impossible for you to focus your attention, so that, try as you might, your attention wanders. My "knowledge" of your being able to focus is probability knowledge—my perception is likely to be true. But this kind of statistical probability does not qualify as omniscience. If God knows *as a matter of certainty* that I am going to lecture at three o'clock, where is my freedom to refrain from lecturing then? Is my choosing to speak an illusion? For God to be all-knowing makes real, substantive human freedom impossible. If God knows the future absolutely, then God also knows God's future choices absolutely. Such perfect foretelling strips God of any freedom as well, a contradiction lurking within the dominant theological scheme.

Two Views of God: Unchanging versus Becoming

The philosophical conviction that God is eternal, unchanging, and impassible (because to feel is to change) emerges from this welter of omnipotence, omniscience, and omnibenevolence. To change, after all, is either to improve (for God, becoming perfect while previously having been imperfect) or to worsen (by having started as perfect and then becoming imperfect). According to this line of reasoning, God cannot abandon perfection, and God has always been perfect; hence, God must be eternally unchanging. For God to be perfect and unchanging, God has to be beyond time and outside of space. Therefore, God cannot be changed by the choices we (that is, all of creation) make or by the things we do. God was perfect before creation, perfect during creation, perfect after creation—and in that sense, separate from creation, above creation and time, independent of creation.

That static, timeless perfection is not how Jewish traditions portray the Divine, even though that is how many Jewish philosophers tell us we should understand God. Despite the impressive lineage of philosophers (and rabbis) arguing for an immutable, impassible, omnipotent, and omniscient God, the Torah and rabbinic midrashim portray a God who gets angry, who loves, who grieves, who gets frustrated and surprised, and who repents!

> When the blessed Holy One recalls God's children, who are plunged in suffering among the nations of the world, God lets fall two tears into the ocean and the sound is heard from one end of the world to the other—and that is the rumbling of the earth. (Berakhot 59a)

As the philosopher Hans Jonas reminds us:

Such an idea of divine becoming is surely at variance with the Greek, Platonic-Aristotelian tradition of philosophical theology that, since its incorporation into the Jewish and Christian theological tradition, has somehow usurped for itself an authority to which it is not at all entitled by authentic Jewish (and also Christian) standards.[6]

The biblical/rabbinic portrayals of an engaged, relating, interacting God are no surprise to Process thinkers or to traditionally observant Jews, most of whom place religious practice (including text study) above more abstract theological reflection.

Holding Morals over Mystery

The conflict is basic: a God who possesses unlimited power and knows everything yet to come could have chosen to fashion a very different world, or else this is the best of all possible worlds. If an omnipotent and omniscient God knowingly created a world in which babies die in their cribs, a world in which people suffer from malaria and die in midlife, leaving their children orphaned—then God is responsible for that (and every) evil. If God could have prevented the Holocaust and chose not to, it is nearly impossible to consider that God to be good. In the words of best-selling author Rabbi Harold Kushner:

A God of power extorts obedience, but cannot command love. A God who could spare the life of a dying child, who could prevent the earthquake but chooses not to, may inspire our fear and our calculated obedience, but does not deserve our love.[7]

Some Western theologians would rather deny their moral compass than change their theology. When confronted by such a moral outrage, theologians too often hide behind the term *mystery*. Or they assert that God's definition of good and evil is different from our own. If a million babies murdered is not evil by God's definition, then the term *evil* has no meaning. Such an atrocity is surely evil, regardless of the perpetrator.

Rather than cling to this outmoded (and unbiblical/unrabbinic) philosophical notion of God and power, Process Thinking offers a way to recover a biblically and rabbinically resonant, dynamic articulation of God, world, and covenant, integrating that portrayal with contemporary scientific knowledge of the cosmos and of life into a philosophy worthy of our engagement.

Of course, that dynamic understanding of a God discovered in relationship alters our understanding of the world and its beginnings as well. So it is to creation we now turn.

2

Reality and Relationship
Being a Creature in a Constantly
Co-created Cosmos

As we learned in the last chapter, Process Theology offers us a dynamic God
as opposed to the unchanging God of dominant Western thinking.
Process Philosophy extends that awareness of identity-in-relationship
and the notion of dynamic becoming to our understanding of the
cosmos and creation. Creation is no longer a one-time event. It, too,
is a continuing process, of which we are a part.

Process Theology recognizes reality as relational. That is to
say, our perception of the world as apparently independent substances that bang against each other and only interact externally is
a coincidence of our size and our metabolism. It is an adaptation
to our own species' evolutionary needs, but it is not an objective
description of the cosmos or its inhabitants. The cosmos actually
is constantly interacting, constantly social, always in process, and
always dynamic. That relating should sound familiar to any Jew,
because our word for that dynamic relating is *brit*, meaning "covenant." Covenant is always interactive, always connecting, and
always relational. This is just like the cosmos: at a quantum level—
the very smallest level—there are no solid substances bouncing
into each other; there are only probabilities, packets of energy
intertwined in their own uncertainty. At the largest scale, that of
our space-time bubble singularity (or, possibly, the infinitely larger

"sea" of eternal inflation-seething expansion), reality eternally generates new pockets of space-time. Only on one size scale—the middle one, ours—can we speak with any coherence about stable, permanent substances. Even on our size scale it is quite clear that we are always on the way, always changing from who we were to who we will become, along with the rest of our dynamic biosphere, planet, and cosmos.[1]

The Give-and-Take of Science—of Us

We and the rest of creation are not static substances. We—and everything that exists—are events.[2] To grasp our nature scientifically, we must simultaneously embrace different levels of being, despite our propensity, when we think of ourselves, to focus on our conscious level. But our multilayered reality complicates any simple self-identity. If we think about humans as collections of atoms, those atoms do not know when they are part of a particular person, when they are part of the air around us, or when they are part of nearby objects. They float in and out of what we think of as "us" all the time. We are completely permeable. In fact, we do not exist on an atomic level, yet that level is no less real than the level of our conscious thought. On a molecular and even a biological level, we also interact with our environment: inhaling air, ingesting food, absorbing heat or cold, sweating, defecating, shedding hair and skin. On the atomic, molecular, biochemical, cellular, biosystemic, bodily, and even conscious levels, we are not stable substances at all. We are constantly engaging in a give-and-take with the rest of creation, all simultaneously. We are immediately connected to all that came before us, up until this very instant, and with all that exists at this very moment.[3] Each of us contains in ourselves everything that has led to each of us.

Freedom is an inherent quality of the world because the cosmos and its denizens are relational, dynamic processes. The world is always becoming, always facing possibilities, and always making choices. There certainly are constraints on those choices. Past decisions create the context in which we now exist. We each know that in our own lives, choices that we made years ago shape the kinds of choices we have available now. For example, you can choose to stay married to your spouse or not, but having chosen years ago to marry that person, your choices are different from what they would be if you had not made that particular choice. We always make our choices from the particular context that is the sum total of our previous choices, the sum total of the world's previous choices. Yet we are more than the mere totality of our previous constraints. The future remains receptive to the decisions we have yet to make.

Meeting God in the Moment

The world, then, is partially self-created and self-creating, and Process Thought acknowledges this. The cosmos is a partner with God in its own becoming. We are partners with the cosmos and with God in our own becoming. We have agency; all creation has standing. The past is offered to us,[4] and God meets us in this moment, as in this moment we come to be anew. Our reality is that in every moment we are coming into being again and again. Think for a moment about the level of electrons, protons, and neutrons at which you are flashing into being, flashing out of being instantly, over and over again. At each moment you are met in the sum total of the choices you made with the choice you now face. Do I attend this college or get a job? Do I marry this person or continue dating others? Do I accept this career path or strike out on that one? You get to decide where you are going to go with each opportunity. That moment of becoming—the present—is called *concrescence*, in which everything comes into coherent being. After you make the choice, the selected option becomes part of God's consequent nature.[5] God holds out another choice to you so that you are free to take or free to reject—and then God meets you in the next choice, with the next possibility. That means that the future is radically open:

Why was this world created through the letter *(hei)?* Because the world is an *exedra* (closed on three sides, open on one): you may proceed if you wish.[6]

Free will is granted to all. If one desires to turn to the path of good and be righteous, the choice is given. Should one desire to turn to the path of evil and be wicked, the choice is given.[7]

God does not and cannot know the future, because the future has not yet been decided. In choosing to create, God made a world that has the capacity to make choices, too. Therefore, Rabbi Abraham ibn Ezra describes God as the One "who can probe all thoughts and see all deeds."[8] Like Ibn Ezra, Process Theology acknowledges that God can only know what is possible to know—past actions and current intentions. In the words of the High Holy Day liturgy, God "knows the secrets of the world"—only what is in the category of knowledge, the revealed and the hidden. The future has not yet been chosen, so it is not something God can know.

Infinite and Finite: The Dipolarity of God

"Lover, indeed, of the people" (Deuteronomy 33:3)—God is the source of the creative, responsive love that pervades the world. Here I want to mention a particularly useful tool that will recur throughout this book. Dominant theology thinks of God in monopolar terms: If God is simple, God cannot be complex. If God is eternal, God cannot be dynamic. If God is perfect, God cannot be in relationship but must exist either at one polar extreme or the other. Morris Raphael Cohen, a Jewish philosopher at the turn of the twentieth century, first articulated the principle of dipolarity, the idea that both A and B can be true if they refer to distinct facets of a phenomenon. So, for example, I can be both father and son, just not to the same person. Process thinkers apply the notion of dipolarity to God and to God's creation.[9] Interestingly, we find this insight in several Jewish sources as well:

Am I only a God near at hand—says the Holy One

And not a God far away?

If a person enters a hiding place,

Do I not see him?—says the Holy One.

For I fill both heaven and earth—declares the Holy One.
   (Jeremiah 23:23)

> In God's greatness and the bulk of God's might, God cre-
> ated the whole world in pairs, each reflection resembling the
> other, and each corresponding to the other. For God made
> them in divine wisdom, to make known that every thing has
> its partner and its reflection, and were it not for the one, the
> other would not be.[10]

Dipolarity is kind of a yin-yang in which we must comprehend both
polarities in order to understand our reality, the fullness of what is
in front of us: "Everything that exists in the world is either of a certain essence or its opposite."[11] This dipolarity extends even to God,
who is infinite in some respects and finite in others. For example,
God is infinite potential prior to creation and in essence even during
creation, but manifests aspects that are finite once entering into relationship with us. Some early rabbinic wisdom expresses that dipolarity in different names for the Divine: *Elohim* for God's absolute
eternity and limitlessness, and *Adonai* for God's entering into the
welter of time and relationship with all creation.

> The word *Elohim*, the designation for God in that same first
> verse of Genesis, refers to a contraction. Since God is endless,
> the creation of the world had to involve a contraction of the
> light, so that God might enter the lower worlds. God remains
> infinite, and the worlds cannot contain God, but since God
> desired their creation God so self-contracted, as it were, that
> they could bear to contain God. It is in this aspect that God
> is called *Elohim*.[12]

As Rabbi Menahem Nahum of Chernobyl points out above, God is separate from creation in some respects and, in some respects, part of creation. The prophet Isaiah proclaims, "Holy, holy, holy—the Holy One of Hosts, God's presence fills all the world" (Isaiah 6:3). God is not separate. God cannot fill something from which God is radically distinct. One can only fill it by being in it, by being co-extensive with it. A useful illustration might be filling a pitcher with water: this is made possible by the reality that the pitcher, the water, and I exist within the same space-time, are made of the same components, and are thus in important ways ontologically continuous. Were that not so, the connection between me and the pitcher, the pitcher and the water, would be impossible. One cannot pour water from a different space-time bubble into a pitcher in this one!

In Pesikta De-Rav Kahana we find, "There is no place lacking the Divine Presence" (Piska 1:2). God is not separate from space-time; God permeates it. God fills it, as the Talmud notes, "God's presence is in all places" (Bava Batra 25a). That means that God is eternal in some respects—God's reliability, God's being the steady source of creating, absolutely eternal—and dynamic in some respects. Recall that God's static eternality is ontology, the study of being. God's dynamism is hyathology, the study of becoming.[13] The details of God's creating—once we move away from the abstract to the concrete—are always incomplete, in process, on the way: "Whatever was created by God during the six days of creation needs further improvement" (Genesis Rabbah 11:6).

Ever New and Renewing: Reality for the Divine and Us

Apparently, this ability to exceed previous perfection—to be vulnerable to creation and open to change—encompasses the Divine as well. For example, in the very beginning of the book of Genesis, after God fashions humanity, we are told that "the Holy One regretted having made people on earth, and God's heart was saddened" (6:6). What does it mean for God to regret and feel sorrow? A timeless, unchanging God cannot regret. *Regret* means being different than you were a moment ago. So the Torah itself asserts God's dynamism in the context of relationship. Over and over again the Torah emphasizes a God who expresses emotion, who meets people in relationship, and changes because of that relationship. God, for Process Theology, is manifest as the ground of novelty. God is to be found in the fact that a universe that is established through fixed, changeless propensities still generates novelty all the time: new unprecedented things that did not previously exist. And, in Process Theology, God shares in the experiences of all creatures and is experienced by all creatures:

> The essence of divinity is found in every single thing—nothing but it exists. Since it causes every thing to be, no thing can live by anything else. It enlivens them; its existence exists in each existent. Do not attribute duality to God. Let God be solely God. If you suppose that *Ein Sof* (Without Limit) emanates until a certain point, and that from that point on is outside of it, you have dualized. God forbid! Realize, rather, that *Ein Sof* exists in each existent. Do not say, "This is a stone and not God." God forbid! Rather, all existence is God, and the stone is a thing pervaded by divinity.[14]

Nothing that happens escapes God's perception and experience, and we are always in touch with the Divine. In Genesis Rabbah 1:10, we learn:

> From the first day of creation, the blessed Holy One longed to enter into partnership with the terrestrial world, to dwell with God's creatures within the terrestrial world.

Our reality is such that God is our partner, dwelling in the world. This is a statement that no contemporary theologian could make, but with which the Rabbis are content. "God is the place of the world, but the world is not God's place" (Genesis Rabbah 68:9). God permeates the world. God dwells within the world.

God not only dwells in the world, but invites all creation, and the human creature, into relationship. The energy of that unfolding relationship charges through humanity, distilling into scripture, ongoing commentary, and the ever-renewing, ever-growing corpus that is the harvest of relationship, of covenant.

3

Change, Choice, and Gift
The Dynamic Nature of Covenant

Process Theology recognizes that the future has not been decided or determined in advance. It remains our privilege to discern the Divine's optimal possibilities and to make choices that advance or get in the way of that best option. What is God's role in how we make those choices? How does God extend that relationship into conversation and content?

The dominant Western way of thinking about God's involvement in our choices posits a bully in the sky who compels behavior or results from unwilling, passive agents or who restrains behavior and precludes outcomes that sinning creatures would otherwise pursue. A key shift for Process Theology is that God does not exercise such coercive power. Rather, God exercises persuasive power. Process Thinking asserts that God works through persuasion and invitation, through persistently inviting us to make the best possible choices, then leaves us free to make the wrong choice. The instant we have made our choice, God persistently urges us toward making the best possible subsequent choice.

In exercising this persuasion, God does not break the rules to force a desired outcome, but instead works with and through us, with and through natural propensities. Here is timely assurance from Midrash Tanhuma:

All might, praise, greatness, and power belong to the Sovereign of sovereigns. Yet God loves law. It is the custom of the world that a powerful tyrant does not desire to do things lawfully. Rather, he bypasses law and order by coercing, stealing, transgressing the will of the Creator, favoring his friends and relatives while treating his antagonists unjustly. But the Blessing Holy One, the Majesty of majesties, loves law, and does nothing unless it is with law. This is the meaning of "Mighty is the Majesty who loves law."[1]

The Lure and Choice

The ancient Rabbis decontextualize this verse and construe it to teach that when one talks about God's might, one celebrates God's willingness to live within natural propensities, or law. Process theologians agree. God does not "break" the laws of physics, chemistry, biology, or morality. In that wondrous way, God's power is not simply an amplification of human power but qualitatively superior and unique.[2] God establishes and works within the constraints of those parameters. The way God works on us, in us, and through us is called the "lure"—what Process philosopher Alfred Whitehead calls the "initial aim"[3] and what Hans Jonas describes as "the mutely insistent appeal of [God's] unfulfilled goal."[4] That is to say, at this very moment—and at every moment—God meets each of us and all of creation, offering us the best possible next step. We have the opportunity and the freedom to decide whether to take that best possible next step or not. That next step—the initial aim—becomes for us our subjective aim, what we choose to do.

We know what the initial aim is. We know it intuitively because we prehend it, Whitehead's term for immediate, internal intuition. We do not have to be told; we are each connected to all and to the creative-responsive love that God offers. So we intuit the lure from the inside. Sometimes we choose not to make the right choice or not to do the right thing because of other forces that impinge upon us: our physicality, drives, selfishness, desires, or laziness. We offer a wide array of excuses for our subjective aim perverting God's initial aim, which leaves God in covenant, hence vulnerable:

> When Israel performs the will of the Holy One, they add strength to the heavenly power. When, however, Israel does not perform the will of the Holy One, they weaken (if it is possible to say so) the great power of the One who is above.[5]

Here again we meet a dynamic, relating God who suffers, a God who becomes vulnerable in having created us. This is not an all-powerful, impassible, eternal God, but a God so connected through relationship that the best way to describe this temporal, passionate covenant partner is in the language of love and law.

Love, Law, and the Consequence of Choice

Lawfulness is itself understood to be a manifestation of love. The prophet Hosea understands this, when he speaks on God's behalf to Israel:

> *I will espouse you forever:*
> *I will espouse you with righteousness and justice,*
> *And with goodness and mercy,*
> *And I will espouse you with faithfulness.*
> *Then you shall know the Holy One. (Hosea 2:21–22)*

The Rabbis recognize this passage as the very heart of the relationship binding the Jew and God, inserting it into the morning liturgy to be recited as the traditionally observant Jew wraps the bands of *tefillin* on the hand in preparation for the morning prayers. To be in covenant with God is akin to marriage: "See, God's love for you is like the love of a man and a woman" (Yoma 54a).

To love someone is to become vulnerable to his or her choices. It is to suffer another's pain, and to exalt in the lover's triumph. It is to want to be steadily a partner and helper, and to sometimes be hurt by the partner's rejection or bad choices. In such a way, God suffers and rejoices in the world and with the world: "In all their troubles God was troubled" (Isaiah 63:9). In Psalm 91, we are told, "I will be with him in his suffering" (91:15). In Mishnah Sanhedrin 6:5, Rabbi Meir says, "When a person is sorely troubled, what does the Shekhinah say? She says, 'My head is ill; my arm is ill; I am not at ease.'"

Just as our suffering pains God, God is diminished by our not rising to make the best choice. The God of Israel is not merely an unchanging, external perfection (although there is an aspect of God that is unchanging and eternal). Rather, we encounter the Divine in the dynamism of *brit*, covenant. There is a dynamic interconnection between God, humanity, and all creation. That interconnection changes how we understand life's big questions—and the choices we make in response.

4

Continuous Creation

Process Theology and the Metaphors of Our Origins

Dominant theologies of creation offer a truncated narrative, imposing a certainty and an objectivity that empirical knowledge does not mandate. One of the advances of Process Theology is encouragement to take a pluralistic approach to understanding creation, that is, to embrace the idea that creation cannot be fully explained by a single theory or fully explored using a single approach. It asks us instead to approach knowledge in a spirit of humility, relationality, and dynamism.

The Scientific Limits of Human Understanding

At least from the medieval period to the present, scholars have remained aware that there is no way to step outside the cosmos to verify or disprove many of our theoretical explanations, no way to prove a definitive, single, all-encompassing account of the Beginning. As tenth-century Jewish philosopher Saadia Gaon notes:

> The problem dealt with ... is one on which we have no data from actual observation or from sense perception, but conclusions which can be derived only from postulates of pure reason. We mean the problem of the origin of the world. It cannot be grasped by the senses, and one can only endeavor to comprehend it by thought.[1]

While it is certainly true that contemporary scientists have "seen" a great deal more than the premodern natural philosophers—background cosmic radiation, galaxies, and nebulae extending to the visible cosmic horizon, for example—it also remains true that we cannot explore and test various space-time bubbles; we cannot step outside of our own cosmos to compare and contrast it with others.

Furthermore, we are limited to an intuitive sense that pertains to our range of size and our durations of time.[2] For size ranges vastly larger than our own (planets, galaxies, space-time) or vastly smaller (molecules, atoms, atomic particles, quanta), human intuition and logic are not reliable. We have not evolved to cope with such enormity or smallness. Nor do our commonsense perceptions function intuitively with the briefest quantum time intervals or with the expansive duration of cosmic events. In such durations and sizes, the only effective system of human relation and expression (constrained by our scientific knowledge) is the five M's: math, meditation, metaphor, music, and myth. Each provides a syntax and narrative to link our consciousness and existence to those realms of reality vastly larger or smaller than our own size range or vastly shorter or longer than the time frames we are evolved to recognize and intuit.

Consequently, when contemplating the possible origins of this universe, Process Theology throws us back to a similar position as the medievals—mustering all available evidence and then generating plausible explanations based on our own presuppositions and use of human reasoning.

Refusing to Ignore the Unformed Darkness

Instead of thinking of creation as *ex nihilo*, out of nothing—as if there were nothing existing previous to creation and then, in an instant, everything suddenly existed—as much of dominant Western theology does, Process Theology takes a more developmental view. I think it fair to say that most Process theologians, beginning with Alfred Whitehead (and myself included), understand God as the organizing force of an eternally existing reality. Such a view surprises those who restrict their view of creation to the first and third verses in chapter 1 of the book of Genesis:

> When God began to create heaven and earth…. God said: "Let there be light"; and there was light.

They ignore the second verse—"the earth was unformed and void, with darkness over the surface of the deep; and wind from God sweeping over the water"—and creation images from elsewhere in the Bible,[3] Midrash, and Kabbalah. The dominant view filters Genesis telling through a preexistent ideology of an omnipotent, eternal, impassive Deity, forcing readers to constrain the text within the procrustean confines of an effortless, spontaneous moment that created everything that exists today. Such an approach conflicts with fundamental scientific evidence, such as the age of the planet, the cosmic materials out of which life is constructed, the fact that living things have developed from previous living things, and the several mass extinctions that punctuated life on earth prior to the appearance of today's species, to mention only a few. Equally significant, such a theological imposition depends on, as mentioned above, ignoring the second verse of Genesis. So much for taking the Bible literally!

A contextual reading of the opening verses of Genesis yields the recognition that the unformed and void darkness (*tohu va-vohu*) existed when God began creating. That bubbling, irrepressible depth remains the source of self-creativity, potentialities, and resistance to all imposed power.[4] God's creating is not necessarily one of instantiating *ex nihilo* from without, but rather a process of mobilizing continuous self-creativity from within:

> An epiphany enables you to sense creation not as something completed, but as constantly becoming, evolving, ascending. This transports you from a place where there is nothing new to a place where there is nothing old, where everything renews itself, where heaven and earth rejoice as at the moment of creation.[5]

The Divine Lure and Our Partnership with God

In Process Thought, every moment *is* a moment of creation! This richer view of continuous creation, it turns out, is also reflected in Jewish sources, beginning with the Beginning itself. The book of Genesis begins with the word *breishit,* which the New Jewish Publication Society version correctly translates as "When God began to create heaven and earth" (1:1), with God's spirit fluttering over preexistent *tohu va-vohu.* Chaos is already there, God sweeping over its surface, and then God begins to speak it into increasing order and diversity. By the end of the first chapter of Genesis, God has spoken creation into a symphony of diverse becoming.

At each stage of the blossoming process of creating, God turns to creation itself and issues an invitation, a lure: Let there be [whatever], and let it flourish according to its own laws, *l'mineihu.*[6] God invites creation to be a co-partner in the process of creating. It is not that God, once and for all, speaks everything that currently lives into existence from the outside. God coaxes, summons, and invites the sun, stars, and planetary objects into becoming. The earth distinguishes oceans and dry land, then generates plants, which cascade into increasing a diversity of grasses, shrubs, trees, and vegetation. God invites the earth to spring up as animal life and then asks each species to continue its own internal growth by its own inner logic— *l'mineiha,* after its own kind.[7] It is worth noting that God sees creation as a process with developmental stages, each with its own integrity and each worthy of celebration. At the end of each day, "God saw that it was good."[8] At the creation of humanity and the beginning of the Sabbath, God "found it very good" (Genesis 1:31). As religion scholar Robert Gnuse notes:

> The statement that God found the creative act of each specific day to be good is highly important, for it means that at each stage of the creative endeavor God stopped and took account of what was unfolding. Perhaps the text even speaks of divine pleasure exhibited at the end of each individual creative act.

If we focus on this language in Genesis 1, we may see the cosmic creation as a dynamic, evolutionary process.[9]

We are told in Tractate Hagigah 12b (and in the morning liturgy) that God "renews every day the work of creation." Creation, then, is not a single intervention with a clear temporal beginning and a sharp conclusion, after which it is complete. The Talmud is suggesting that God constantly creates, indeed permeates the process of creating. The Zohar, the keystone text of the Jewish mystical tradition, extends this idea even further. It quotes from the book of Proverbs, "By understanding God continually established the heavens" (3:19), and asks: What does the phrase *continually established* mean?

> God goes on arranging the *sefirot* every day, and never stops. They were not arranged at one particular time, but God arranges them daily because of the great love and the pleasure that the blessed Holy One feels for them and for their preciousness in God's sight.[10]

Creation, then, is the process of God luring emergent being into order, abundance, diversity, and goodness. That means there can be no break with natural propensities at any point in the process. God works with and through material reality. The universe is not merely passive stuff that God molds into shape; it is a co-creating universe.

> God created the world in a state of beginning. The universe is always in an uncompleted state, in the form of its beginning. It is not like a vessel that the master works to finish; it requires continuous labor and renewal by creative forces. Should these cease for only a second, the universe would return to primeval chaos.[11]

God permeates that *tohu va-vohu* stuff and expresses through it the ability to live:

The activating force of the Creator must continuously be present within the created object, to give it life and continued existence.... And even as regards this physical earth and its inorganic components, their life-force and continued existence is the "word of God." ... There is a kind of soul and spiritual life-force even in inorganic matter such as stones and dust and water.[12]

Understanding Creation: Two Options

There are two contemporary scientific ways to contextualize the process of continuing creation we have described, each accepted at present by large segments of the scientific community. Each provides plausible accounts of the data we have at present, and each leaves certain large assumptions unproved and unprovable in theory. The two plausible options correspond in broad outline to the two medieval cosmic options—an eternal creation and a creation of space and time as part of the creative act.

Eternal Inflation

Eternal inflation asserts that our space-time bubble is located in a cosmic "sea" of infinite, eternal inflation. This "sea" is sometimes referred to as the superuniverse, the multiverse, or the meta-universe.[13] Within the eternal inflation, only quantum rules govern, although on rare occasions due to long-shot quantum odds, exceptional space-time bubbles emerge into being within which expansion does not pertain. Within each bubble there is a coherent space-time, and we live in one such bubble. So what we think of as the Big Bang and all of existence, in this understanding, is really one space-time bubble in an infinite sea of eternal inflation that erupts into other new space-time bubbles. In this eternal realm, neither space nor time have meaning—time because it has no direction, and space because it is the same in every direction and in every place. Of course, this eternal inflation, existing beyond space-time, is unverifiable and immeasurable in principle. It lies beyond human cognition or description, in a realm of math, meditation, metaphor, music, and myth (where, as mentioned earlier, all human conceptualization and meaning making occur).

Big Bang Theory

Big Bang theory starts with the instant in which space-time exploded into existence, that primal singularity some 14 billion years ago that created the vast cosmos in which we live, move, and exist. The Big Bang itself is held to be inexplicable; the regularities of physics fail as we move back in time the singular moment itself. Within that singularity, we can only marvel at the remarkable fine-tuning of the major forces of the cosmos, a slight variation of any of which would have made life impossible.[14]

These two understandings of creation—an infinite, eternal, inflationary multiverse or a singular Big Bang—may be disturbing to people who have read the Bible exclusively through dominant theological lenses, but Jewish traditional voices provide the resources to accommodate both. So let me offer a passage from Ecclesiastes Rabbah, which quotes from Ecclesiastes 3:11, "As God has made everything beautiful in its time":

> Rabbi Tanhuma said, "In its due time was when the universe was created. It was not proper to be created before then; it was created at the right moment." (Ecclesiastes Rabbah 3:13)

Assuming there is one universe, it was created at the right moment. If you prefer to think of the cosmos as co-extensive with our space-time bubble (and there are plenty of scientists who do), Rabbi Tanhuma and many other Sages share your view. There is no way for us to stand outside of our space-time bubble to test whether there are other space-time bubbles, let alone an infinite and eternal expansion. Those people who posit multiverses are driven by logic and existential preferences, not by experience. They may be right, but we will never know with certainty.

But that same midrash goes on to say:

> Rabbi Abbahu said: "From this we learn that the blessed Holy
> One kept on constructing worlds and destroying them, until
> God constructed the present one and said, 'This one pleases
> Me, the others did not.'" (Ecclesiastes Rabbah 3:13)

The second part of the same midrash expresses the idea of an infinite
number of universes, of which ours is only one. Apparently ours is
not the first generation to speculate on the possibility of previous,
perhaps infinite, universes. These rabbinic Sages, like their Process
progeny, were comfortable understanding God the Creator as having
created not only once, but as the God who is always creating.

Must We Choose?

About these two choices—an eternal inflation with repeated space-
times or a singular space-time that encompasses all—individual
scientists have strong preferences, but science as a whole does not
definitively weigh in on this issue. We are left with two conceivable possibilities, each scientifically plausible and each religiously
compatible with the understanding of creation as an ongoing process presented by biblical and rabbinic sources. We are (still? once
more?) in the position that Maimonides explicated in his magisterial
Guide of the Perplexed:

> It was to our mind established as true that, regarding the
> question whether the heavens are generated or eternal, nei-
> ther of the two contrary opinions could be demonstrated.[15]

God may be the One who creates everything out of nothing or the
One who creates order out of eternity and infinity. Process Theology
saves us from having to weigh in beyond what we can know. We can
indulge in a little dipolarity here, rather than asserting a false certainty. Instead of creating a false dichotomy between the two plau-
sibilities, we can embrace both understandings as useful metaphors

to orient and motivate ourselves within the cosmos. In either telling, God continually lures this dynamic creation, working in, with, and through all that exists to generate greater order, expressiveness, diversity, and abundance.

Life and the Experience of Evil
Process Theology's Eye-Opening Approach to Tension, Trauma, and Possibility

If God is not the coercive despot who created all as it is, if God is found in the steady relational love that invites creation into diverse becoming, what then is evil?

As we have learned, in the dominant theology, an omnipotent, omniscient God becomes the source of our suffering, either actively, by commission, or passively, by refraining from intervention. In either case, it is easy to feel abandoned, betrayed, or persecuted by such a coercive power. In such a theology, evil is a conceptual conundrum to be rationalized through better reasoning or to be evaded through redefinition.

Process Theology offers two possible understandings of evil, both facing the tragic nature of evil directly and affirming the innocence of those who suffer. One view addresses evil as that aspect of reality not yet touched by God's lure or that part of creation that ignores God's lure. Another Process approach to suffering and evil draws on the thought of medieval Jewish philosopher Moses Maimonides, who acknowledges that much of what we term *evil* or *suffering* is a matter of perspective. Maimonides, speaking out of the naturalism that Aristotelian thought makes possible, points out how often what we term *evil* is simply our perspective on a particular event:

> The ignoramus and those like him among the multitude consider that which exists only with reference to the human individual. Every ignoramus imagines that all that is exists with a view to his individual sake; it is as if there were nothing that exists except him. And if something happens to him that is contrary to what he wishes, he makes the trenchant judgment that all that exists is an evil.[1]

In Process Thought, much of what we understand to be evil is the very source of dynamism and life. Our planet is churning, so that the rocks do not settle in order of heaviness, but the heavy ones keep getting kicked up to the surface. That is why there is life on the surface of the earth. Were it not for the tectonic activity of the core, there would be no life on the surface of this planet. Events that are disasters for some are sources of emerging novelty and development for others. So the process of evolution is driven precisely by a tension between limits, on the one hand, and possibilities, on the other. Maybe that is why Isaiah says that God is the One who "makes peace and creates evil" (Isaiah 45:7).[2] God has to be *borei ra*, the Creator of evil, because out of what is experienced as evil comes life itself. We cannot have one without the other.

The Three Realities of Suffering

As we learned in our examination of the Process perspective of continuous creation, the cosmos itself does not follow a predetermined script. Every level of the cosmos follows its own inner dynamic—always facing possibilities, always making choices—and therefore is in the process of becoming, as are we. As Maimonides explains in Process fashion, most human suffering, what we deem *evil*, is not divine punishment or test, but the result of three broad realities of life.

That's Life: The Nature of Being Human

The first reality is that it is the nature of material reality to come into being, to grow and flourish for a time, and to then fall apart prior to going out of existence:

> The first type of evil is that which befalls people because of the nature of coming-to-be and passing-away. I mean to say because of our being endowed with matter. Because of this, infirmities and paralytic afflictions befall some individuals either in consequence of their original natural disposition, or they supervene because of changes occurring in the elements, such as corruption of the air or a fire from heaven and a landslide.[3]

This realm of suffering is the logical manifestation of dynamism and change. The only alternative, a world of static eternity, is one that few of us would choose—even if it meant embracing an alternative that also brought suffering and death. More importantly, we do not have that choice, which is Maimonides's point. Dynamism, hence suffering and death, is built into the very nature and logic of materiality.

Tyrannical Domination: Imposing Bad on the Good

It is also possible to understand large swaths of suffering and evil as the result of our freedom, the freedom of the entire cosmos. Sometimes we individuals, or humanity at large, make bad choices, and sometimes the rest of the cosmos makes disastrous choices. This accounts for the next category that we perceive as evil and experience as suffering as described by Maimonides: "The evils of the second kind are those that people inflict upon one another, such as tyrannical domination of some of them over others."[4] This category of evil requires no additional supernatural intervention, but is the immediate result of our freedom and our relatedness.

The Consequences of Our Freedom

The third and final category of evil and suffering is related to the second: our freedom to make poor choices also means that we inflict harm on ourselves when we do not muster the strength and vision to heed the divine lure, what Hans Jonas describes as "the mutedly insistent appeal of [God's] unfulfilled goal." Again Maimonides:

> The evils of the third kind are those that are inflicted upon any individual among us by his own action.... This kind is consequent upon all vices, I mean concupiscence for eating, drinking, and copulation, and doing these things with excess in regard to quantity or irregularity or when the quality of the foodstuffs is bad. For this is the cause of all corporeal and psychical diseases and ailments.[5]

The dynamic, ephemeral nature of becoming, the competing lures that tempt us and distract us from God's lure, the consequences of our choices on others and ourselves—these remain sources of suffering and evil: the consequence of poor diet choices or too many sweets, lack of regular health regimen, bad choice for companionship or community. Process Theology allows us to recognize their sources as proximate, within nature, and not as the judgment or punishment of the Divine. In turn, this realization allows us to continue to perceive God as our ally and source of strength in times of tribulation, to be able to reorient ourselves to focus receptively on implementing the divine lure before us, to freely choose to affirm those relations (and make those choices) that bring us strength, joy, and health.

Process Theology opens our eyes to a biblical-rabbinic-kabbalistic view of God as relational and loving. "I am with you, declares the Holy One" (Haggai 1:13), working in, with, and through us to bring order to the chaos in our lives and societies, giving us the strength and insight to know how to struggle for health, connection, and justice.

Moving Beyond Thinking to Action

Understanding God as the pervasive creativity and novelty that permeates all-becoming invites us to stop *thinking* about the status of evil and to focus instead on how we fight for justice, well-being, and compassion. *"You shall love the Holy One your God* (Deuteronomy 6:5)—this implies that one should make God beloved by one's deeds" (Nedarim 81a). Evil and suffering are not intriguing theological puzzles; they are existential goads, calling us to repair the world. This shift from intellectual justification to action has ancient precedent. The Rabbis perceive God as preferring righteous behavior to correct belief: "Would that they had rather forsaken Me but maintained My Torah, for the great light emanating from the Torah would have led them back to Me" (Nedarim 81a).

If we are part of creation, and if we also have the ability to align ourselves with the divine lure, then evil is a summons for us to implement justice, which is resolute love. What choices must we make now to obviate evil tomorrow? That question beckons as a revelation: What is it that God asks of us?

The Process of Revelation
Spiritual *and* Cognitive,
Primal *and* Verbal

Revelation is a term that embraces a range of responses, conveying the sense that God communicates with creation. Both in hints and traces scattered throughout creation (nonverbal) and through the testimony offered by scripture (verbal), Judaism joins with many wisdom traditions in affirming that we can discern the Divine and implement a sacred agenda. Note that for Jews (and Christians and Muslims), revelation involves two interrelated challenges. We need to clarify whether, and in what ways, the Divine enters into communication with us. And, as a distinct but related matter, we want to specify the ways that particular scriptures and traditions convey divine communication. In philosophical language, the former is the challenge of universal revelation (discernment of the Divine available to all through nature, intuition, and reason), which Judaism calls *gilui ha-Shekhinah*. Special revelation (made accessible through particular scriptures and tradition) is known in Judaism as *matan Torah*, giving of Torah, or as *Torah min ha-Shamayim*, Torah from heaven.

Does God communicate to us at all? Does God "speak" to us through nature? Did God give us a Book to guide us? Are the words in that Book God's or ours? What is the relationship between the Book we now possess and the content God wants us to possess? Does God speak to us now? Is God's communication limited to the Book, or are there other venues as well? And in what ways might that Book and its traditions be authoritative? These questions emerge anytime a sensitive person tries to perceive God's presence and will, either in the welter of life or in the context of Torah.

It turns out that our different assessments of revelation fuel a great deal of human conflict. Many people reject revelation not because they reject a coherent imperative emerging from being alive in the cosmos, but because of the shackles placed on that broader idea by the conventional metaphysics of mechanistic reductionism (that the cosmos is a big machine that can be explained completely by the interaction of its smallest components). Construing the world as composed of solid substances that interact externally and, further, defining God as outside and separate from natural reality force us to choose between stark dichotomies: Is the Bible human or divine? Does God speak authoritatively through the Sages or not? How does a timeless God of Spirit enter into an ephemeral world of materiality? One of the great gifts of a Process perspective is to liberate us to go beyond these dualisms both when we encounter the fullness of the universe and of life, as well as when we read and interpret our sacred writings. As a description of reality and as a hermeneutical tool, Process Thinking creates a possibility for a renewed relationship to life and an embrace of Torah and tradition in a way that bridges these gaps and integrates our lives with our highest convictions.

Revelation and the Dominant Metaphysics

Within the framework of the dominant substance metaphysics, we are forced to understand the world as composed of two distinct categories: natural substances—subject to space, time, motion, and change—and supernatural things—simple, eternal, and unchanging. The key questions this metaphysics forces us to ask are these: How does the supernatural enter into the natural? What are the mechanics for how the eternal, the spiritual communicates with (and imposes its will on) the temporal, the physical? This challenge applies both to an eternal God acting on a physical universe and to a spiritual soul directing the actions of a carnal body. Most denominational battles can be mapped by their response to this single divide.

There are only three logical possible resolutions for how an "up there, out there" timeless spirit can communicate to the "down here" physical, changing world:

1. That communication can be detailed and accurate, meaning each and every word is God's completely. Of course, this option assumes that God speaks perfectly within one particular scripture (its own!) and treats all other scriptures as merely human or, at best, inferior.

2. That communication can reflect our human perception and projection, so each and every word is completely human.

3. Or the communication could be in some way a mix of the two distinct participants, with some passages reflecting divinity and others expressing a human perspective or context (although in fairness, this third position merely postpones addressing the core incompatibility of the two realms).

If the words are purely God's, then their authority is pretty strong and would supersede shifting social norms or personal preferences. If the words are purely human, then they might contain literary nuggets, but they would be advisory at best, and most likely would become outmoded with increasing antiquity. If they are some mix of divine and human, then the challenge would become how to distinguish between which passages are divine, hence of abiding value, and which verses reflect the limitations of an earlier age.

Indeed, that three-part division of logically possible responses parallels Jewish denominational divisions, too. Within Judaism, for example, much of Orthodoxy believes that an eternal, omnipotent God spoke words that were accurately recorded, chronicling historical events and presenting true biographies, in the Bible and in Rabbinics. They further assert that the Sages accurately interpret those books to be able to rule on the application of God's will in every instance. Those premises make the authority of Torah and its interpretations binding, specific, and absolute. Most Reform thinkers across the centuries affirm that the Bible—like all great compilations—has a natural history, and consequently have restricted God's will to the ethical values in scripture, categorizing the rituals to the human growth of the ages. Authority shifts from the Book and tradition to each individual conscience and what wisdom each person might perceive in any particular law or narrative. Conservative thinkers have affirmed a middle position without great clarity: somehow the Book has a natural history yet remains authoritative. Jewish law is both evolving and obligatory. So under Conservative views, Jewish practice and tradition are embraced as positive, modified only when necessary. This leaves Conservative practice rich in building community and meaning, yet straining to discern which parts of the tradition retain abiding wisdom (hence, authority) and which parts require new formulation to best reflect contemporary understandings of divine values.

Note that all three responses keep God's character and involvement categorically distinct from those of humanity while reducing revelation to a discrete set of verbal propositions, accurate history to be affirmed, true ideas to be accepted or rejected, and laws to be implemented correctly (or to be violated). The dominant model creates a sense of revelation that emphasizes true belief (dogma) and timeless standards of behavior. It also creates a self-justifying yardstick for affirming one's own scripture as divine while denigrating or ignoring all other sacred writings. Ritual practice becomes an easy way to locate someone along this denominational spectrum; as a result, ritual practice becomes the shorthand for particular Jewish identity. Ethics and moral standards become less significant than affiliation and belonging, often receiving less public emphasis or attention. This hierarchy of true ideas and binding practice may diminish the importance of intuition and emotion by placing a more brittle and rigid distillation of ideas as the litmus test of religious propriety: heaping stringencies on dietary rules that make it more difficult for realitives to gather together, or forcing Galileo to swear that the earth doesn't revolve around the sun, despite the evidence. In itself, this prioritization of religious observance over ethics renders religion less attractive and less adaptive to many. As Process Thinker Alfred North Whitehead notes:

> Religions commit suicide when they find their inspirations in their dogmas. The inspiration of religion lies in the history of religion. By this I mean that it is to be found in the primary expressions of the intuitions of the finest types of religious lives. The sources of religious belief are always growing, though some supreme expressions may lie in the past. Records of these sources are not formulae. They elicit in us an intuitive response which pierces beyond dogma.[1]

By viewing revelation as the written historical record of timeless truths, the individual person and the actual event recede into the background and the proper application of timeless principle emerges as primary. Widows are burned on their deceased husbands' funeral pyres, Jews and other indigenous peoples are massacred in crusades or inquisitions, and children are sacrificed to idols in the scenario of abstract principle taking precedence over actual people and real moments. Much of the tragic history of religious conflict—indeed, of any ideological conflict—can be traced to this monstrous inversion erected on the foundation of dominant metaphysical assumptions.

Of course, there is another way, bringing to the fore and questioning the metaphysical axioms that permitted that inversion in the first place. By rejecting the primacy of being over becoming, of abstract and timeless truth over actual lives and real experience, Process metaphysics can liberate us to live our lives with stronger relationships and greater justice. In the remarkable words of noted Process theologian Catherine Keller:

> The spirit in which we journey is a spirit in process. And so divinity itself—that which we can name or conceive as "God"— will be discerned in process. "Discerning divinity in process"

carries a double meaning: our theological images shift, diver-
sify, and evolve; and that which we imagine *in* those images is
discerned to be a living process. *Process* ... means *becoming*: it
signifies the intuition that the universe itself is not most fun-
damentally a static being or the product of a static Being—but
an immeasurable becoming. Indeed the word *genesis* in Greek
means "becoming." The God of a universe in process may in
powerful ways turn out to be a God in process: that is, in open-
ended interactivity with each of the gazillions of us creatures.
For the divine process, if we can imagine it at all, is infinite
and therefore inexhaustible. The traditional unchangeables of
God may prove to be points of theological fixation rather than
fixities of a divine nature. They may be the false fronts of our
cultural immobilities: "God or Unchangeable Absolute" func-
tions as "Sanctioner of the Status Quo"—even if that status
quo is unjust and unsustainable.[2]

In what way can Process Thought clarify our understanding of revelation? How can Process Theology assist us in making sense of the
proposition that we can communicate with the Divine and discern
God's purpose with reliability? How can a Process perspective open
up for us the real wisdom of biblical and rabbinic writings (as well as
the wisdom of other scriptures) to enhance and elevate our lives and
societies? And how can a Process approach enable us to discern the
lure within scripture and identify the immoralities that an infantile,
passive acceptance of scripture often supports? It is to these questions that we now turn.

Process Theology: Universal Revelation

Let's recall some of the key understandings of Process Thought.
Rather than enforcing a strict division of natural and supernatural,
Process Thought affirms that we live in a *uni*-verse, a single integrated
reality. Nature is far more mysterious and awesome than most of its
spiritual detractors or materialist manipulators concede, so there is
neither evidence nor necessity for a realm beyond it (which may be

why neither the Bible nor Rabbinics have a term for *natural* or a term for *supernatural*). Everything is in dynamic relationship with everything else. Indeed, existence is "becoming-in-relationship." God is not timeless and separate from creation. God is the One who offers us the best possible options for our own future and who lures us to attain the divine goals of maximal relationship, engagement, love, compassion, and justice. God uses persuasive, persistent power to allow us to intuit the optimal choice for each of us and empowers us to be able to make that choice, should we so choose. And God works in and through all of creation, at every level, inviting every aspect of creation to respond affirmatively to the divine lure uniquely appropriate to it at that precise moment. God does not break the rules, but works to create a cosmos in which flourishing is possible.

This understanding of revelation is not restricted to a particular book (or any books) or a particular tradition (or traditions). There is no interaction lacking in God's gift of insight, purpose, and direction. There is no occasion that does not invite our choosing the optimal response unique to us. No new reality can emerge that does not engage both partners in this timely and recurring partnership.

Those insights permit us to bypass much of what religions argue about (and sometimes kill over). If God permeates creation and works within and through creation, then the question is no longer "Does God communicate?" since in some important ways everything can be a manifestation of divine-creaturely communication, as the psalmist notes, "The heavens declare the glory of God" (Psalm 19:2). Similarly, the medieval poet Rabbi Shlomo ibn Gabirol anticipates the philosopher Immanuel Kant when he recognizes,

> *Three things meet in my eyes*
> *To bring Your remembrance before me always:*
> *Your heavens—I recall your nature*
> *And they are my faithful witnesses,*
> *The place I dwell, which arouses my thoughts*
> *With its expanse, which recalls the expander of my pedestal,*

And the musings of my heart when I look within my depths.

In every occasion, my being blesses the Holy One forever.[3]

God's glory is not restricted to words, but is found in the starry skies, in the planet Earth, and in the poet's own conscious awareness. Later mystics attest to that same insight: "All that people see—sky, earth, and its fullness—are God's outer garments, manifesting an inner spirit, the Divine which permeates them."[4] God is manifest in all. Guided by this renewed insight, we can seek God in the world, in each other, in our own interiority. Hikes, hugs, and quiet contemplation offer moments of *gilui ha-Shekhinah*, occasions of universal revelation to those who approach the cosmos, each other, and themselves with receptive wonder and expectant silence.

Nor do we need to ask the impact a pure Spirit has on a carnal materiality. God already permeates each and every one of us, and every component of this interacting creation, in our distinctive uniqueness and our diversity. We, too, can recognize the Divine in the concrete diverse garb of creation. As the medieval poet Abraham ibn Ezra notes:

I see You in the starry field,

I see You in the harvest's yield,

In every breath, in every sound,

An echo of Your name is found.

The blade of grass, the simple flower,

Bear witness to Your matchless power.[5]

Everything in creation may be a manifestation of divine action and invitation *and* a manifestation of creaturely agency and self-determination. God is not a radically different visitor or intruder from another order of being, but the soulful presence permeating all. Because "no place is devoid of the Divine Presence" (Exodus Rabbah 2:5), all significant acts of invention, insight, and inspiration are the upwelling of the divine invitation and the human (or other creature's) response. However, keep in mind that not everything that happens is revelatory. Only those events that optimize love, justice, compassion, relationship (in other words, events that embody God's lure) offer a revelatory possibility. Through that interactive model— of God's lure and human responsiveness—Process reveals all revelations to be. It emerges from relationship, and each of the partners contribute their share.

One more aspect of universal revelation invites our notice. The Divine Presence is a gift God offers to all seekers, to any questing person, to all creation. This manifestation of the Divine itself, not contained in any distinct set of words, is available to all. Beyond words, nonverbal in its receipt, this aspect of revelation opens through relationship itself, Presence to presence. "There is no utterance, there are no words, their sound is not heard. Yet their shout rings throughout the earth, their words to the end of the world" (Psalm 19:4–5). This mode of revelation is universal because it is not borne by particular cultural symbols, distinct human languages, memories, or festivals. Instead, biblical tradition itself affirms a more expansive, pervasive revelation of God through creation itself. All humanity can claim access to the Divine in this way; all creation is linked in living fellowship to its One Creator and to the rest of creation itself. Like all meaningful relationships, this one is sustained through empathy, imagination, play, memory, experience, and fantasy. Summoning the human arts of feeling, touching, and reaching out, this mode of revelation embraces the integrated whole of who we are as living beings, as mammals, as humans. We need not *read* this revelation, and it does not *speak* words. Instead, we open ourselves to the starry skies and the awesome wonders of nature, we recognize the divine image in our fellow human beings and connect emotionally to that image in each other, and we nestle within our own interiority, there pulsating with the holiness we find. This is a revelation accessible through struggles and celebration, through tears and laughter, through art and meditation. This revelation, nested in a root deeper than speech, cradles our loving embrace: God, world, self.

Process Theology and Special Revelation

Consider that biblical tale in which universal revelation meets special revelation. Responding to the plight of the Israelite slaves, Moses is leading the children of Israel from bondage under Pharaoh. Now in the wilderness, he seeks an intimate awareness of God. He pleads with God, "Let me behold Your Presence!" (Exodus 33:18). Notice that Moses doesn't ask for a definition, for a verbal response, for a law code. He asks to see God's presence. And God responds favorably, although with a caveat: "I will make all My goodness pass before you, and I will proclaim before you the name the Holy One, and the grace that I grant and the compassion that I show. But," God said, "you cannot see My face, for humans may not see Me and live" (Exodus 33:19–20).

Moses pleads for *gilui ha-Shekhinah,* a universal revelation of relationship deeper than any words. To that request, God accedes. What God promises to show Moses is both *dynamic* (God agrees to pass by) and *protective.* God promises to shield Moses during the most intense encounter. What Moses is capable of grasping—what Alfred Whitehead would call *prehending,* to emphasize its intuitive and non-verbal character—is all about relationship, interaction, empathy, and justice; God's "goodness," "grace," and "compassion." What Moses cannot prehend is God's ontology, the nature of God's being as it is on its own. That limitation poses an insoluble puzzle to the dominant theology, but Process resolves the challenge quite clearly: none of us have access to a kind of being that is not also becoming. Being on its own is a (mere) logical abstraction. It is only being in relationship to others, that is to say, becoming, that can be apprehended, that can enter into relationship. God is no exception here; none of us are knowable abstractly, through some distilled definition. All true knowing is relational and dynamic, for us *and* for God.

Thus far, the revelation Moses requested and God promised is universal revelation: nonverbal, the gift of connection and relationship, available to all through imagination, emotion, vulnerability. But that moment swiftly transitions into special revelation, the distinctive distillation of relationship into speech, the universal into the syntax and symbols of a specific language and culture. God passes by Moses and what emerges, along with the dynamic motion, are words: "The Holy One passed before Moses and proclaimed, 'The Holy One! The Holy One! A God compassionate and gracious, slow to anger, abounding in kindness and faithfulness...'" (Exodus 34:6). In that instant, the exchange takes the contours of particular words, in the context of a specific language—Hebrew. No longer universal, this encounter is distilled into a form directed specifically to Israel: a specific name nestled in a particular relationship.

The wonder of this story lies to no small degree in its refusal to separate the two modes of revelation. They are not so neatly distinct, are they? Asked to reveal intimacy and connection, God does that and more. God also speaks words that form the core of the Rosh Ha-Shanah and festival liturgy in Jewish worship across the ages. Presence and relationship, speech and behavioral norms are all fused in this wondrous narrative. Maimonides shares his wonder at this potent brew:

> Moses's request regarding the knowledge of God's attributes is conveyed in his saying: "Show me now Your ways, that I may know You." Consider the wondrous notions contained in this dictum. For his saying, "Show me now Your ways, that I may know You," indicates that God, who is exalted, is known through God's attributive qualifications; for when Moses would know the *ways*, he would know God.[6]

God's presence is manifest in God's ways. The universal cloaks itself in the particular. Indeed, only when cloaked in the particular does the universal make room for distinctiveness and diversity. The implication is that every path of wisdom is a garment for the One. Not just Judaism, not just Western faiths, but all wisdom traditions offer a particular take on something beyond the mundane. And the diversity of the garb is essential. Otherwise, universalism is merely the polite face of smothering conformity, the gracious imposition of power. Not so the revelation offered here: universal and particular come together. Verbal and nonverbal mingle in every moment. God's presence is prehended by observing (and imitating) God's ways. Yet those ways also erupt into words. As the medieval philosopher Hasdai Crescas makes explicit, revelation is both "a spiritual and cognitive overflow from God to humans."[7]

Spiritual *and* Cognitive, Primal *and* Verbal

Sensitizing us to look for dipolarity, Process Thought prepares us for that fusion. But it also invites a deeper insight. In recognizing that God and the world are not separate dichotomies, we recall that the world is permeated with God, who at each moment offers all elements of creation the optimal choice for their particular situation and concern, while also providing them with the capacity to make the choice that is optimal for each one. In our capacity for self-determination, we are not only co-creators with God but also co-revealers. There are aspects of God that are separate from creation (and from us), but there are also aspects of God that permeate creation and constitute our best. Beyond merely translating Presence into Word, a Process understanding of revelation insists that these are not distinct modes but complementary perspectives of an embracing whole, not shifting realities but interacting aspects of a dynamic series of events. In the dance of universal and special revelation, the godliness within expresses the Godliness we discover, and in that meeting, new intuitions, new possibilities, sometimes new words emerge. Just as blossoming can never remain abstract but must always result in an actual bloom, special revelation is a blossoming of universal revelation in particular flowers.

Process Theology sees the world as a single realm, with every event in a process of interactive becoming. There is no timeless realm of static spirit, but rather spirit is a process that emerges from the agency and relatedness of every creature. Because God works through the reality of the world as it is, like creation, revelation takes place within a natural framework. God reveals through us. But Process moves us beyond even our previous notion, a revelation in which some parts are God's and other parts are human. Process insists that revelation is 100 percent God and 100 percent human, that the two percentages frame different perspectives on a single, integrated distillation of words. The entire Torah is divine. The entire Torah is human. No longer do we need to remove the undesirable words or phrases; now we must rise to the responsibility of interpreting the text in such a way that God's love, justice, compassion, and connection become more apparent, more inspiring, more clear. Revelation involves active engagement, not passive reading.

Note that this is precisely how the ancient Sages, the prophets and Rabbis of old, did their work of creating midrash, rabbinic interpretations of biblical text, to spin new golden threads of *aggadah* (legend) and *halakhah* (practice). Process illuminates the courage of the ancient Rabbis and lures us to rise to their level of responsibility and creativity in our own era.

Approaching Judaism and Jewish tradition through this perspective accentuates a rich textual support for God dynamically engaged in every level of creation, passionately urging us to ethical greatness, social justice, inclusive diversity, and a deep spiritual practice. Hence we need no longer battle over whether scripture is divine or human. It is the Divine manifesting *through* the creation; it is humanity verbalizing God's lure. God speaks through human words, and our best insights articulate the Divine; as the Zohar expresses it, "The Shekhinah speaks from the throat of Moses" (Zohar 3:234a).

For Jews, the Torah represents the supreme distillation of this divine lure and human agency into words. Torah neither simply dropped from the skies nor is exclusively the invention of human fancy; Process allows us to integrate our reverence and love for this particular text while honoring its actual history. God reveals continuously; everywhere and anytime, it is possible to discern the sacred and intuit an optimal next choice, often perceived as an imperative. That revelation can emerge as a verbal expression, and in Torah, it is indeed the harvest of generations of Israelites who listened faithfully and distilled their insights into stories and laws. To the degree that their attentiveness is an expression of God, to the extent that God guides their discernment, to the degree that their ethical reach reflects God's breadth of vision and depth of love, to that degree the Torah we actually possess is inextricably human *and* divine. As with every other aspect of existence, the fusion is pervasive and irrevocable.

In this instance, the Torah's having a natural history answers historical and literary questions: How did this book come to be? Who wrote its components? Who compiled and edited it into a unitary collection? The Torah might even address the question of original intent: How would these verses have reverberated in an ancient Near Eastern context? These questions are the purview of academic scholars of Bible. Their research has uncovered ample evidence to support the Documentary Hypothesis, which holds that different schools of ancient Israelites each contributed strands that were artfully integrated and woven into the Torah we now possess. That entire process is rooted in Israel's most ancient beginnings and reached literary completion sometime around the First Exile in 587 BCE. The Torah of Israel is truly a collective work: not only does it engage the entire people across generations, but it also articulates the divine potentiality that invites continuing interpretation, exploration, and new tellings of its tales and new applications of its laws.

Torah Wisdom Revealed through the Prism of Process

There are six Process implications that may be made explicit here:

1. *The Torah's history of compilation and editing is best understood through the Documentary Hypothesis, but that method of delivery doesn't preclude our intuition that this Torah is the Torah selected and created by the God of Israel* (matan Torah) *and selected and created by the people of Israel* (kabbalat Torah). *To confuse the method by which the Torah was given with its status as revelation is to confuse literary theory with assessments of value. Knowing what ink Shakespeare used doesn't affect our assessment of the quality*

of *Hamlet.* It is at least as conceivable to perceive God giving the Torah through generations of Israelite Sages across multiple generations as to portray God as dictating a book on the top of a mountain. Indeed, for most people today, it is more credible to understand God giving Torah (that is what *matan Torah* means) through this method of *kabbalat Torah* (receiving Torah). In the words of theologian Rabbi Jakob Petuchowski, "Literary history cannot solve the questions asked by Theology; and the question as to the *fact* of Revelation is a *theological* question."[8]

2. *Because we understand the Torah as the inextricable fusion of the divine and human, giving and receiving Torah is a process without end.* Any process is a series of events across time, and the process of giving/receiving Torah is composed of a series of events arranged chronologically, too. From the first telling of stories that grew into the compilations found in our Torah, from the first standards and practices that have been distilled into the imperatives and prohibitions that are the commandments (*mitzvot*), there has been a steady process of telling, doing, interpreting. These happen all together, in an organic rather than a linear order: all at once, each simultaneously influencing each other and being influenced by each other. Small surprise, then, that some of the stories and several of the laws strike many moderns as horrific: the very values that have emerged from the Bible sensitize us to hear those tales and practices with heightened awareness. Scripture is always clothed in interpretation, made real through active engagement. No wonder that the ancient Rabbis understood that the Written Torah was supplemented with an Oral Torah, the interpretive key to keeping scripture fresh, relevant, and wise. Oral Torah, originating in the same source and with the same level of authority as the Written Torah, makes possible the freshness of God's lure toward engagement, relationship, justice, and compassion. In the words of an ancient rabbinic sage, "Even what an acute student will expound before a teacher has already been given to Moses at Sinai" (Y. Pe'ah 2:4). Sinai is a symbol for an ongoing process without end, not just a particular moment at a particular mountain. Without a push toward

playful interpretation in each age, the Word would calcify into something brittle, foolish, and harsh. Lubricated with the living juices of each new generation and their new discoveries in the humanities, the natural and social sciences, their insights into morality and the adventure of spirit, Torah is renewed and rebirthed in each new reading and every new interpretation. The rabbinic understanding of the dynamic of Oral Torah—ever growing and always the key to fixing the meaning of Written Torah for each particular time and place—is profoundly compatible with a Process understanding and is strongly rooted in the metaphysics that Process articulates.

3. *Faithfulness to the special revelation launched by the Torah requires affirmation of* Torah min ha-Shamayim, *that a cosmic wisdom fuels the very Torah and commentaries given direction through us.* This calls for entering into relationship with the stories of the Torah as reflective of our own human struggles and mission. Affirming *Torah min ha-Shamayim* as it pertains to the commandments requires walking the pathways of Torah's standards as they continue to be applied and as new understandings emerge. Nowhere in the Bible does the text insist that we must believe literally that these narrated events happened historically. Instead, we are instructed to "take to heart these words which I command you this day. You shall diligently teach them to your children. You shall recite them at home and away, morning and night" (Deuteronomy 6:6–7). The obligation is to recount these stories, to weave them into our lives and our generations. For example, the first two chapters of Genesis provide two incompatible chronicles of the sequence of creation; graphing when Moses is on top of Mount Sinai or at the base is impossible based on the book of Exodus; there are two different versions of the Ten Commandments. These inconsistencies are not editorial sloppiness but deliberate signals to the attentive reader. Indeed, the Bible seems to go out of its way to make those two options virtually impossible to reconcile. Like any great poem, the Torah teaches life-transforming insights and offers vitalizing wisdom. In its narrative inconsistencies, the Torah advises us:

"Pay attention to the wisdom in this story! That is the realm in which life-affirming significance can be found. The details are the frame through which the lesson can be taught." As articulated in its introduction, the medieval book of commandments *Sefer Ha-Hinnukh* understands that the reason the biblical narratives were written as they were in scripture is "for the great essence and need that can be found in them." In other words, what the Torah demands is that we affirm these stories' significance, not their putative truth. Indeed, as theologian and author Arthur Cohen clarifies, "any 'fiction' which informs life with greater richness and seriousness is, to that extent, no fiction but reality!"[9] Nowhere does the Bible demand that we practice each imperative or prohibition literally as specified in the Bible. Nowhere does the Bible explicate what *tefillin* are to look like or how they are to be worn. Nowhere does the Torah specify what constitutes labor for the sake of Sabbath rest. The Torah itself creates the need for its own interpretation, to translate *peshat* (the contextual meaning) into *derash* (the significance or implication of a passage) so it can be practiced as a *mitzvah*. In its lists of imperatives and prohibitions, scattered as they are among broad ethical and contextual principles ("You shall have one law for you and the stranger," "I am the Lord your God," "Love your neighbor"), the Torah insists: Your obligation is to fashion lives and communities that reflect these commandments through the core values they seek to establish—human dignity, justice, compassion, holiness.

4. *The Torah is meant to be the first word, not the last.* In good Process fashion, the Rabbis of old speak of the Torah as an *etz hayyim*, a living tree, or tree of life. Just as a tree sinks its roots deep into rich, moist soil to provide stability and water to its leaves, just as it continues to add to its trunk and to expand its foliage, so too does Torah grow and blossom in each age. Rooted in our ancient beginnings and our sacred origins, it too continues to grow and expand to address contemporary concerns, to integrate new insights, and to harvest new wisdom. An ancient talmudic story (Menahot 29b) posits Moses standing on

the pinnacle of Mount Sinai, watching God add little crowns to certain Hebrew letters in the Torah. (If we were meant to believe in the historical fact of the Torah's narrative, how could the ancient Rabbis have dared to make up such an audacious tale not found anywhere in biblical literature?) God explains, "There will arise a man, at the end of many generations, Akiva ben Yosef by name, who will base extensive legal teachings on these little crowns." Moses asks permission to see this wonder, and in an instant he is transported some fifteen hundred years into the future, into the study hall of Rabbi Akiva. The rabbi is presenting a detailed lecture on a technical point of Jewish law, and Moses grows increasingly uncomfortable because he can't follow the discussion and doesn't understand the subtleties. Finally a student asks Rabbi Akiva, "Where did this come from?" and the rabbi responds, "It is a law given to Moses at Sinai!" The narrator tells us that Moses is comforted to hear this. What makes that response so wonderful is that Moses couldn't understand the debate and clearly had never heard of the legal nuance Rabbi Akiva was explicating. Yet the fact that this future rabbi (two thousand years prior to us) rooted his arguments in interpreting Torah, and credited his innovations to the process launched by Moses so long ago, gives Moses joy. That continuity and living process should give us joy, too, and empower us to read boldly, willing to make the interpretations needed in our own time for God's love and justice to shine more brightly through our words of Torah.

5. *Ethics takes precedence in the Torah.* Understanding revelation through the perspective of Process Thought restores an ancient priority, often diminished in modern times—the priority of the ethical over the ritual in Jewish tradition. This frequently comes as a surprise to those exposed to traditional Jewish practice today, but the priority is ancient and runs deep. Dividing the commandments into two categories, *mitzvot bein adam la-Makom* (commandments between people and God) and *mitzvot bein adam le-havero* (interpersonal ethics), the Bible and the Talmud clearly place the ethical over the ritual. Two examples

will have to suffice: On Yom Kippur, the most ritually punc-
tilious day of the year, the Rabbis selected as their prophetic
reading the stirring passage from Isaiah 58:1–12, in which the
prophet berates his contemporaries for oppressing the weak and
the poor while thinking that their precise performance of sacrifices somehow makes them right with God. They wonder why
God seems to ignore their fasts and sacrifices, and they are told
the reason in no uncertain terms:

> *Because on your fast day you see to your business*
> *And oppress all your laborers!*
> *Because you fast in strife and contention,*
> *And you strike with a wicked fist!*
> *Your fasting today is not such*
> *As to make your voice heard on high.*
> *Is such the fast I desire,*
> *A day for people to starve their bodies?*
> *Is it bowing the head like a bulrush*
> *And lying in sackcloth and ashes?*
> *Do you call that a fast,*
> *A day when the Holy One is favorable?*
> *No, this is the fast I desire:*
> *To unlock the fetters of wickedness,*
> *And untie the cords of the yoke*
> *To let the oppressed go free;*
> *To break off every yoke.*
> *It is to share your bread with the hungry,*
> *And to take the wretched poor into your home;*
> *When you see the naked, to clothe them,*
> *And do not ignore your own flesh.* (Isaiah 58:3–7)

Isaiah isn't opposed to ritual, but he is militantly opposed to some
of his contemporaries' despicable shows of ritual attentiveness
while still oppressing and marginalizing other human beings. At
the center of Isaiah's call to return to Torah standards is his insis-
tence that fashioning societies of justice and compassion is our
core religious commitment and that ritual (important though it

is) plays a secondary role to ethical rigor. That the Rabbis of the Talmud advance this biblical priority is clear from their selection of this passage to be read on Yom Kippur and from countless times in which ritual practice is superseded by ethical concerns— for example, creating a technical method for liberating slaves when the Bible explicitly forbids it (Berakhot 47b, Kiddushin 22b, Gittin 40a and 43b), and creating a technical way to bequeath property to daughters, despite an explicit biblical prohibition (Ketubot 68a). There are countless examples of rabbinic activism in which the Sages of Israel harness the tools of legal analysis and interpretation in the service of the ethical values that infuse the Torah to this day.[10] Their subversion of precedent in the name of ethics was undertaken in the service of Torah and seen as an act of both faith and loyalty. As the Talmud observes (Yoma 69b), "Why did those Sages abolish what Moses had ordained? Rabbi Elazar replied, 'They know that the Holy Blessing One is truthful and would say nothing untrue about God.'" We can do no less if we wish to advance the religion they practiced. Reading Torah through the lens of Process Theology restores this clear biblical/ talmudic imperative to its rightful place.

6. *Process Theology stresses pluralism in practice.* Because Process Theology affirms that God meets individuals in the specificity of their own uniqueness at each particular moment, we affirm that for each person, for every created event, there is a lure distinctive and unique. No two moments offer the same opportunity, and no two individuals stand in the same situation with identical needs. Each lure is uniquely tailored to the optimal outcome for that individual at that moment. But the encompassing goals remain the same: greater experience; greater relationship; greater justice, compassion, and love. How those values are put into practice is where differences emerge. So too with translating Torah into life: no two communities face the same situation with identical collective memories, priorities, shortcomings, challenges, and opportunities. How the living reservoir of Torah and *halakhah* are applied, then, will be different for each different individual and for every community: "They [communities

following different practices] do not disagree. One master rules in accordance with his locale and the other master rules in accordance with his locale" (Yoma 55a). It is for precisely this reason, to create room for a pluralistic implementation of shared revelation and values, that we learn that *halakhah* follows the most recent authority[11] and that judges can only rule according to what their own eyes see (Niddah 20b). A Process understanding of revelation accounts for the historical and contemporary reality of robust diversity in how different communities implement Jewish law and practice, across time and in different geographic locations. Pluralism is built into the particularity of how the lure is offered and how it is received. As with any legal system, the diversity of legitimate practice is a source of communal vitality and legal continuity. The Torah is viewed in such a way as to best meet the ongoing needs of each particular community and to advance the holiness and ethics of each new age.

Revelation's Implications for Today

This Process understanding of the nature of revelation carries powerful implications for our own day. In denying that God, in a single instant and in isolation, authored the specific words in the Torah, I do not mean to belittle either God or God's Israelite partners in revelation. On the contrary, I am asserting that no book, however insightful, can possibly contain the complete and final lure of God for each of us and for all humanity. God's fullness and love are dynamic and specific, always requiring new expression and new commitment.

Jewish law represents the continuation of that love affair in history between God and the children of Israel. It incorporates a sensitivity and insight for holiness as only something ancient and precious can. Because of that preciousness, it retains its lure and authority for us as well. Through Jewish law, itself dynamic and evolving, Jews come together to integrate the raw and nonverbal aspects of universal revelation with the emerging words and positions of special revelation that can, in turn, radiate holiness and purpose back into our lives, our communities, our world.

Halakhah is a process through which we can wrestle each other to achieve some measure of consensus. In good dipolar fashion it is also how we can celebrate diversity while setting the limits necessary for our *brit*, our covenant, to thrive into the future. As with the Torah, it is impossible to say where the human element in *halakhah* stops and where the divine begins. Rather, we can say that *halakhah* is the shared effort of the Jewish people and God to make the light of goodness, justice, compassion, and love visible in the world. Just as light can only be seen when it bounces off a physical object, so too holiness can only be shared and encountered when it is embodied in social and communal structures. The key question is not "What does the Torah say?" but rather "What does God tell us through the Torah?" Providing answers to that existential question is the lifelong task and privilege of every Jew, as is answering the comparable question for every seeking soul within his or her own tradition.

Our task as seeking, questing people, every day of our lives, is to live in the presence of God and to mediate that presence to the larger world. In the words of the psalmist (Psalm 16:8), "*Shiviti HaShem lanegdi tamid,*" we must set God before us always. The process is endless, the lure is great, and the moment is now.

Death and Afterlife
Two Paradigms of Hope
and Enduring Significance

As it was in the beginning, so it shall be in the end. Our stories of beginnings took advantage of dipolarity to embrace two plausible scientific/mythic tellings: Big Bang *and* eternal inflation, each redolent of biblical, midrashic, and kabbalistic imagery and insight. Each of these narratives takes us beyond the limits of empirical understanding, although they are each constrained by current scientific knowledge to reflect a minimal standard of plausibility. Now, turning to questions of death and afterlife, we seek yet again to peek behind the curtain, where certainty and knowledge cannot arbitrate. Process Theology joins Jewish tradition in offering two plausible paradigms. Rather than the false swagger of pretended certainty, as viewed through dominant theology, we can embrace the openness of aggadic hope and multiplicity, knowing that truth flashes just under the surface of such narratives.

Death and Patterns of Energy

A Process perspective on death and afterlife affirms the same speculative metaphysics as all Process insight: we generally think of ourselves as substances, but we are actually organized patterns of energy. Everything is in flux, everything is dynamic, everything is volts of electricity—which is to say, a great light that was fashioned at the beginning and hidden away. As we serially flash in and out of existence, on every level, we are free to determine our next choice, constrained only by our previous choices and the choices of the rest of choosing creation. God does not know the future. God knows objectively and retains forever all that has already occurred. One of the ways God changes is by integrating and responding to our choices and actions. After we are offered the initial aim—God's best possible option—we then select our subjective aim, choosing what we prefer to do. That choice, and its subsequent series of events, then becomes eternally part of God. God's integration of those events is eternal.

Process Theology allows us to formulate a plausible understanding of life in the coming world (*olam ha-ba*). *Olam ha-ba* is the biblical/rabbinic term for our continuing as objectively real aspects of God's thought. We are not substances now in life, and we will not be substances after life ends. We are patterns of energy now, and it is reasonable to believe that we will continue as patterns of energy in God's eternity.

Afterlife and the Many Possibilities

At this point, however, the specifics of the nature of that continuing existence diverge, for Process Theology and for classical Jewish texts as well. Judaism posits belief in eternal life. The Talmud insists that one who will not proclaim the prayer for the resurrection of the dead is immediately removed as prayer leader (Berakhot 26b, 29a), and Maimonides lists affirmation of the afterlife as one of the core required beliefs of historical Judaism.[1] Beyond affirming faith in some form of continuing existence, however, Jewish wisdom is remarkably open. As Rabbi Louis Jacobs writes:

> Religious agnosticism in some aspects of this whole area is not only legitimate but altogether desirable. As Maimonides (1135–1204) says, we simply can have no idea of what pure spiritual bliss in the Hereafter is like. Agnosticism on the basic issue of whether there is a Hereafter would seem narrowness of vision believing what we do of God. But once

the basic affirmation is made, it is almost as narrow to project our poor, early imaginings on the landscape of Heaven.[2]

This religious realism permeates Jewish theology—affirming what we can, and specifying only when possible. In this instance, Judaism affirms an afterlife, but refrains from specifying a single vision of that future. Value-concept terms—such as *gan eden* (Garden of Eden), *pardes* (paradise), *gehenna* (hell), *olam ha-ba* (the coming world), *t'hiyat hameitim* (resurrection), *gilgul ha-n'shamot* (reincarnation), *keitz ha-yamim* (end of days), and *yeshiva shel maalah* (supernal academy)—circulate in various Jewish conceptions of afterlife but are never defined with precision or authoritatively. Using the building blocks of these value concepts, many different conceptions of life after death abound within religious Jewish traditions. Those options remain viable for a Jewish Process thinker.

Once our lives are finished and done, we continue to exist—as we have lived—on multiple levels. All the stuff of which we are composed continues in the world. The atoms that constitute us do not vanish with our death. Our proteins are recycled in the ongoing cycles of life. Everything that we are gets reused and continues.

One possibility is that death marks the end of our individual consciousness. Our energy patterns continue unabated, but there is no governing central organization, no self-reflective awareness that continues beyond death. In such a possibility, we merge back into the oneness from which we emerged. We go to sleep as discrete individuals and awaken as the totality of the cosmos.

A second possibility builds on the first, adding the plausible hope that consciousness and identity continue unimpaired. As God is process, and as God is the One who is supremely connected to everything, supremely related, and forgetting nothing, we remain eternally alive in God's memory, in God's thought—which, it turns out, is what we have been all along.

Part II

Process Theology and Jewish Life

With the completion of part 1 and its presentation of the principal ideas of Process Theology, we now turn, in part 2, to a more audacious claim. There have been many streams of thought within Judaism, and competing schools and approaches have all made valuable contributions to the totality of Jewish heritage. Now I want to advance the claim that a Process approach provides a rich hermeneutical framework through which to unlock hidden layers of meaning within biblical/rabbinic Judaism, to burnish rich resources of significance, and to make greater sense of many of the structures and claims of historical Judaism. Process Theology enables us to establish a robust relationship to Jewish scriptures and practice in a context of personal integrity, with openness to contemporary knowledge and insight, and with an emphasis on spiritual depth and social engagement. There are significant ways in which an optimal vision of Judaism emerges through the lenses of Process Thought.

Process Theology may seem new and unsettling at first, but part 2 shows that much of Judaism is, in fact, inherently Process. It begins with an act of reclamation. Instead of ceding the primacy of love to any other faith, Judaism boldly insists on love at its core and then implements that love personally and communally, through *mitzvot* of spiritual intimacy and social justice. Chapter 8 will detail the many ways that a Process approach makes the centrality of love clear, and chapter 9 will locate that love in the realm of corporeality—living bodies and a physical cosmos.

Chapter 10 will advance this argument, showing how the embodiment of meaning emerges in relationship, linking our lives in compelling communities and enacting that encounter with covenant at every stage of life. Chapter 11 will revisit the notion of *mitzvot*, the sacred commandments of Judaism, asking how we can integrate a notion of behavioral imperative that enhances our lives, encourages intellectual curiosity and candor, and celebrates our distinctiveness and diversity. Chapter 12 takes those insights into the heart of revelation and the ways in which God and humanity work together as co-creators to make meaning and advance an agenda of ethical rigor.

Chapter 13 addresses the emotionally charged place of Israel in contemporary Jewish identity, using Process methods and insights to fashion a more stable and profound relationship with Zion and with everywhere Jews live, thereby modeling ways that all people can relate to particular cherished places and to the holiness of the entire planet Earth.

Another knotty religious issue is that of prayer, addressed in chapter 14. Process Thought offers a tool to understand what it is we are doing when we turn to God in speech, song, and contemplation and also helps make sense of what God is doing in response. Chapter 15 similarly uses Process insights to help us make sense of why tragedies happen and what we can do to respond to them, as individuals and as caring communities.

Mortality, the notion that all living things cease to exist, poses a challenge that threatens to erase all efforts at meaning or even effort itself. In chapter 16 we will explore ways in which a Process understanding of the dynamic of birth, life, and death can extend our sense of meaning beyond the limits of our own life span, planting our significance in more extensive soil.

Finally, with chapter 17, we turn to that greatest of contested gifts, the freedom of all becoming entities. Gifted with an open future, one in response to our own self-determination, we will explore how Process Thought invites us to make wise choices to optimize our future and to advance God's aspirations.

The Power of Resilient Love
The Persuasive Persistence of Loving-Kindness

A few years ago I received a package in the mail from Professor Thomas Oord, a Christian theologian who teaches at Northwest Nazarene University in Idaho. He mailed me two of his latest books because he had read an article of mine and he thought they would help us launch a conversation. The two books offer an extended argument that the central virtue of Christianity ought to be love—not faith, not salvation, but love. Reading his insightful books, *Defining Love* and *The Nature of Love: A Theology*, it occurred to me that the subject is one that has a natural home in Judaism and calls for a Jewish reclamation. I want to make a Process Theology argument for why, as Jews, love is important; what it is that Jewish love entails; and how we might foster a more persistent and resilient love to heal this broken world and to bring wholeness to shattered hearts. The key insights and connections made possible by Process Thought will make this position viable and vital.

Dominant Hate Transformed by Emergent Love

Love is the central reality of Process Thought. Everything that exists does so in relationship, and all meaning and value are the lived experience of relating to each other. The most profound underpinning of those relationships is love, which inspires creation, resolves conflict, and generates new life. God relates to humanity primarily through love—the inviting power to surpass ourselves and to risk growth and innovation. Indeed, God's vulnerability and dynamism are both a manifestation and a consequence of God's love for us and for the world. Recognizing that all living creatures are in a continuing pattern of engagement and connection, we become who we are by our courage to love and to nurture. And we, like God, remain vulnerable and self-surpassing because of our resilient loves.

Yet I do not need to tell you that this is a brutal age. All you have to do is peruse the news to know that this era reels from gruesome violence. Vast civilian populations are terrorized in every sector of the globe. At home the political system is stymied by rampant partisan vitriol, as Democrats and Republicans have lost the ability to learn from each other and instead mock each other, yelling invectives across the aisle. We witness examples of humanity's inhumanity in all regions of the world: so-called "honor" killings, terrorism so prevalent that the newspapers no longer use that term to describe the people who assault innocents and murder children. Slavery, which we once thought was relegated to the nineteenth century, is now practiced in most parts of the world, especially victimizing children and women. There is ubiquitous sexual predation; we see bigotry based on sexual orientation, faith, skin color, ethnicity, special needs, or place of origin.

The list goes on and on. People who are assaulted by the violence of others feel increasingly isolated as a result, lacking in community, belonging, and meaning. The cycle spirals out: the more people fear, the more they surrender to hate. The more vulnerable they feel, the more they hate. The more ruthless and unconnected they feel, the greater is their rage and hatred. Adrift in meaninglessness, they confuse hatred for purpose, and multitudes cling to their desperate disdain of those they don't really know as a way of anesthetizing their own fragility. Terrorists and extremists feed on that fear and desperation. They suck strength from the way people feel assaulted, misunderstood, or at risk, causing those people to feel further victimized. The cycle begins again; hate is a process, too.

We Jews know that same reality of hate from our own history, both ancient and recent. We are told that we were slaves in Egypt and outcasts; we know that we were to the Egyptian overlords *to'evot*—abominations—so we caricatured them as idolators and they lampooned us as less than human. We construed our encounter with Egypt as a cosmic battle between good and evil. Throughout the ages an endless series of people have beaten, raped, and murdered Jews simply for being Jews, and that same anti-Semitic distortion and violence continues in our own time around the world. This is true most especially, I believe, in a level of hatred against the State of Israel and in calls for Israel's destruction that can only be characterized as insane. Meanwhile, we Jews also make choices that contribute to the victimization of others, even as we attempt to transcend our own victimization.

The need for love—strong and abiding—is so pressing because the hatred is so widespread. Judaism's response to hatred is to redouble our efforts at love: to be able to love more persistently than those who hate, more resiliently than they fear; to respond to acts of violence with acts of resolute justice; to be able to stand for values of righteousness, decency, and inclusion in places of terror, fear, and exclusion. It is time to reclaim *chesed,* covenantal love, as the imperative of this age, and to assert *chesed* as the central Jewish religious value. *Chesed* is different from *ahavah,* which means, simply, "love." *Chesed* is not simply an emotion burnished on the inside, but an emotion that translates into a sustained loving response. *Chesed* is sometimes translated as "loving-kindness" to indicate this overflow of nurture, support, protection, empathy, and proactive behavior. *Chesed* is the process of embodied loving. Love is as love does.

Love Is the Antidote to Hate

Why is love the antidote to fear and to hate? Scripture tells us, "*olam chesed yibaneh*—I will build this world with love" (Psalm 89:3). The cosmic and biological force for building a new and a better world is love. Supernovae give of their core to spawn new generations of galaxies and to forge the elements that make life possible. Love is the engine that drives life's expansion toward greater complexity and consciousness. Love is the catalyst for the creation of new generations. Mammalian parents cradling their young understand the redemptive power of love. Children clasping the arms of an elderly grandparent understand the redemptive power of love. We read lyrical, liturgical poems of love in our houses of worship, and secular and religious people alike resonate to the creative efforts of artists across the centuries who share their love in music, sculpture, drama, and words.

Only when we feel valued, recognized, and affirmed can we take the risk to see the humanity of the people around us. Jewish tradition understands that insight. Knowing that we have been chosen by God is precisely what gives the Jewish people our resilience, generosity, and fortitude. It is only through a proactive, dynamic love that we can, in fact, become open to the needs of other people, to affirm their humanity, however much they may belittle their own.

A story is told of Rebbe Moshe Lieb Erblich, one of the great Hasidic rabbis in the late 1700s, who is also known as the Sassover Rebbe:

> The Sassover Rebbe enters an inn, and sits beside two local peasants. As the two peasants sit at the bar and drink, they begin to fall into a drunken stupor. One turns to his comrade and says, "Tell me, friend, do you love me?" His colleague responds, "Of course I love you. We're drinking companions. Naturally I love you." Then the first one said to his friend, "Then tell me, friend, what causes me pain?" His colleague said, "How should I know what hurts you? I'm just your drinking buddy." He said, "If you loved me you would know what causes me pain."[1]

From that day on, the Sassover Rebbe taught his students that to love another human being means to know what causes that person pain, to know what makes that person suffer or hurt. It is but a small step from knowing what it is that causes someone's heart to break to mobilizing to alleviate that pain.

Another story about the Sassover Rebbe:

> It is told that on the holiest day of the year, Yom Kippur, the Sassover's congregants were sitting in the shul waiting for the services to start—but no rabbi. One woman decided that she was close enough to her home that she could leave the synagogue quickly, check in on her child, make sure that he was safe and comfortable, and then she could rush back; no one would notice. She ran home, opened the door to her hut, and there, sitting next to her child's crib, was the rabbi, cradling the sleeping child in his arms. He looked up at her and said, "I was rushing to get to shul on time, and I heard crying coming from your house. As I entered the house I saw that your child was awake and scared. So I rocked him in my arms and we sang together until he fell asleep. By then I had forgotten what day it is today."[2]

What kind of a great tradition tells a story about a rabbi who forgets that it is Yom Kippur? What an amazing heritage that recounts the tale of a *tzaddik,* one of the righteous, who thinks that rocking a baby to sleep is more important than leading services! What a wonderful example of Process Thought's love as engagement and connection at the heart of our own tradition! What a beautiful and wise pathway to understanding that it is in holding each other, in singing together, that we fashion the kind of world in which we aspire to live. Perhaps that is why *Shir Ha-Shirim,* the Song of Songs—the greatest love song of all time—and the book the ancient Rabbis tell us is the Bible's most sacred, teaches us that "love is as strong as death, and as mighty as Sheol" (8:6).

In an age teeming with merchants of death, people who seek to impose a living hell on their fellow human beings, we must respond with a redoubled love (*ahavah*). We must love stronger than they hate. We must love longer than they hate. We must teach them that our *chesed* will be the antidote to their poison.

Chesed: Covenantal Loving-Kindness Is a Process

Judaism understands love, *chesed*, to be covenantal—the dynamic and persistent integration of the inner emotion and virtues of affection, empathy, desire, yearning, and delight with deeds of *tzedek* (justice), *shalom* (wholeness/integrity), and *berakhah* (blessing/well-being). As the Process perspective reminds us, it is always about relationship. Love takes place between two parties, not internally within a single individual. *Chesed* is dynamic, meaning it is always changing, open to integrating new insights from the world and the covenantal partner. It is persistent, just as Process teaches of God's love. Love does not back down; it neither retreats nor surrenders. That definition is a mouthful, and it will reward us to analyze its component parts in turn.

Jewish Love Is Covenantal and Alive

Covenants are not necessarily restricted to equal parties. Kings and vassals are not equal, yet they provide the sociopolitical context for the biblical covenant. God and the Jewish people do not claim to be equal. But they do insist on the ability to bridge the chasm of disparity with relationship, and in relationship you may stand as a partner even with someone who is not your equal. As the Talmud reminds us, "The Holy Blessing One does not deal like a despot with God's creatures" (Avodah Zara 3a). Love spans the gulf, which allows unequals to stand in partnership and in dignity together, despite their differences; indeed, *because* of their distinctiveness. The entire Jewish tradition is a recurrent outpouring of covenantal love: God creates the world, we are told, in order to have an object to love. As if that isn't enough, God rises up against Pharaoh and brings us to freedom, because God so loves our ancestors. As if *that* isn't enough, God brings us to the foot of Mount Sinai and there offers us a covenantal contract, which the Rabbis tell us is a *ketubah*, a wedding contract. The wedding contract sealing the relationship between the Jewish people and God is the very *Sefer Torah*, the Torah scroll, we read from today. Ours is an ancient tradition of covenantal love.

Strikingly, covenantal love is very different from popular culture's portrayal of love, the pitter-patter of a heart that only lasts as long as it takes to toast a bagel. Five minutes later, our attention drifts to some other infatuation. So we live in a culture with all these romances, passionate beginnings, and frequently volatile finales. We read about the various celebrities and their love affairs, and we read about their breakups and their new love affairs. That superficial, provisional appetite is not covenantal love. Covenantal love, we are told, nurtures understanding and generosity—seeing the best in your lover, your children, your community, humanity, and the world—then, with similar generosity, sharing in their struggles and efforts.

Jewish Love Is Dynamic and Persistent

Such covenantal love is both dynamic and persistent, just as Process understands God's loving, and our own. Along with being misunderstood as a fleeting fad or passion, covenantal love is also sometimes taken to be an objective assessment of priorities. Between the incinerating heat of passion and the icy chill of judgment, there is no room for a love that thrives. Jewish love is alive, which means it is always open to change, always in relationship. As the philosopher Franz Rosenzweig reminds us, "Love brings to life whatever is dead around us."[3]

Nobody can be in a relationship without being open to change. Ask any parents, and they will affirm that what their child needs from them is different now than it was a year ago. And it will be different, thank God, a year hence. Love changes when it finds need for change—a responsive vulnerability—but it must also be persistent. When your child presents you with a challenge, your love will sustain the child, providing the strength to overcome that challenge. That yearning for life, for wholeness and connection, allows us to withstand life's disappointments, pain, and brutality.

Jewish Love Integrates Our Inner Emotions with Deeds

Chesed is the integration of values and emotions with deeds or action. One of the defining characteristics of every living creature is homeostasis, the ability to maintain a consistent, internal environment despite an external environment that changes. That ability to integrate is the hallmark both of being alive and of having character. Love is the ability to integrate all our powerful emotions in consistent, empathic behavior. Our emotions inspire us to act. Our actions hone and temper our feelings. The cycle is never static and never ending. The spiral of feeling to behavior to elevated feeling to ennobled behavior rises us toward infinity. "I love [*ahavat*] you," says God, "with an everlasting love, therefore I continue my loving-kindness [*chesed*] to you" (Jeremiah 31:3).

Love (*ahavah*) ripens as loving-kindness (*chesed*), primarily in three clusters:

Tzedek, **justice.** The symbol of *tzedek* is the scale evenly, tentatively balanced. Judaism understands that love and justice are not conflicting values. They are dual expressions of one core value, as light is both particle and wave. Indeed, Judaism affirms that love is the source and the root that nourish justice, while justice is the fruit and the flower of determined, abiding love. Jewish tradition reminds us, "You shall not oppress a stranger, for you know the feelings of a stranger, having yourselves been strangers in the land of Egypt" (Exodus 23:9). Or, in sage advice attributed to the ancient Jewish philosopher Philo, "Be kind, for everyone you meet is fighting a great battle." We know that *chesed* results in acts of caring and justice. Covenantal love is not weak; it does not tolerate a world in which there are no rules or consequences. *Chesed* is resolute, strong, insistent, and fair.

Shalom, **peace.** Moving beyond the simplistic, *shalom* means so much more than merely "peace." *Shalom* comes from the Hebrew word *shalem*, which means "wholeness, integrity." The Jewish philosopher Baruch Spinoza writes in his *Political Treatise* (chapter 5:4), "Peace is not the absence of war; it is a virtue, a state of mind, a disposition for benevolence, confidence, justice." Love must be grounded in the entirety of who we are—our memories, character, experiences, body, temperament, and aspirations. Our love must also be grounded in our integrity—in the authentic selves we are in private and in public. As the Hasidic master Rabbi Simcha Bunim told his students, "You cannot find peace anywhere if you do not find it in yourself."[4] The wholeness and integrity of *shalom* means not making yourself small because others would have you shrink from your own greatness. *Shleimut*, wholeness, means offering to the world the fullness of who you are at your best: your beauty as you are, your greatness as you are. *Shleimut* means inviting others to rise similarly to their unique greatness. Jewish tradition understands that the value of *shalom* is an act of love so significant that it is nothing less than messianic. It will advance the age of universal harmony if we practice *shleimut* with resolute determination: "If you fulfill the law of kindness to birds, you will fulfill also the law of freeing the slaves ... and you will thereby hasten the advent of the coming Messiah" (Deuteronomy Rabbah 6:7).

Berakhah, blessing and well-being. There is so much bounty manifest in this world, a harvest we did nothing to deserve. We were simply born into a world that was prepared across the millennia for our arrival. Our task in the world is to savor the bounty, to delight in it, steward it, and help each other to do the same. We are to make ourselves a blessing and commit to being grateful for the blessings. That is why the structure of Jewish prayer always starts with *Baruch Attah*. *Baruch*, in the blessing formula, does not mean "blessed" literally. God does not need our blessing. God is the Source of all blessing, the fount of all bounty. So we start our *berakhah*, our spur to mindfulness, by noting: You, God, are bountiful, *Baruch Attah*. After that general admission we then specify God's particular loving-kindness of that occasion: You are bountiful for giving us Torah ... You are bountiful for giving us life and bringing us to this season ... You are bountiful for giving us bread to eat. Jewish prayer is a resilient discipline reminding us of the bounty of being alive and that we are called to embody God's image. We are called to be like God, sources of bounty and blessing for others: "Be a blessing ... and in you shall all the families of the earth be blessed" (Genesis 12:2–3).

Connecting through a Deeper Love

When we examine the concepts of love, as emotion, as catalyst, as engagement, through the prism of Process Thought, we strengthen our resolve to connect with each other in a deeper love and a more persistent loving-kindness. In a world so afraid that it routinely erupts in hatred, we are commanded to love. In a world in which children go to sleep without knowing that they are safe or that there will be a meal tomorrow, we Jews are commanded to love. In a world in which people believe they can bully the State of Israel out of existence, we are commanded to stand tall for the liberation and national self-expression of all peoples, and to love. In a world in which some go to bed hungry, some go to bed impoverished, some go to bed sick or lonely, we Jews are commanded to know what makes them hurt, and we are commanded to lift them up.

Love works its transformative magic as we grow to love ourselves, body *and* soul. Love spawns the work of social justice as we learn to love our fellow creatures, their character *and* their corporeality. Love emerges as cosmic identification as we work to implement our love for this planet and its denizens in their physical reality. Bodies matter when it comes to love.

9

"The Body Is the Glory of the Soul"
Finding Holiness in the Integration of Spirited Bodies

Jomo Kenyatta led Kenya to independence after years of colonial rule. When asked to explain what he saw as the central dynamic of modern African history, he quoted the old African adage, "When the Europeans came to Africa, the Africans had the land and the Europeans had the Bibles. Then the Europeans taught the Africans to get on their knees and to pray with their eyes closed. When we opened our eyes, the Africans had the Bibles and the Europeans had the land."[1]

President Kenyatta's pithy observation reminds us that many see a split between being concerned with the realm of the spirit (prayer while kneeling, eyes shut, clenching a Bible) and concern with more material objects (bodies, land, and possessions). That split goes to the very core of Western civilization, toward the earliest assertion of an incompatible dichotomy between spirit and body, between an essence of soul and an essence of physical carnality. That chasm affects us to this very day, when we are bidden by many voices to be more introspective and more spiritual. Religious observance of spiritual practices, such as meditation or fasting, underscores an attention to our interior life, calling on us to examine the state of our souls, to do the kind of tough inner work that a life of spiritual discipline demands. But it turns out that there is a better way. Rather than having to take sides between body and soul, we can use the Process insight that the spirit-body dichotomy is false: soulfulness is bodies in process, and embodiedness is how soulfulness manifests. The two are terms for different aspects of human becoming, and one cannot exist without the other. One does not "have" a soul, and a soul is not "in" a body. Process Theology reminds us that we are embodied souls and soulful bodies.

Body, Bad. Soul, Good.

In our age, many consider a spiritual life as superior to a physical life. According to this view, physical things are somehow destructive, biological bodies are somehow less significant, and the core action is in the realm of spirit, somehow distinct from physicality. We owe this dichotomy in large measure to the Greek philosopher Plato and his student Aristotle. Plato taught us that the ideal cannot be physical. A physical chair, while related to all other chairs on some level, is always faulty—it gets scratched, it breaks, it isn't perfectly balanced. But the concept of the chair, the *idea* of the chair—that's where chair perfection is found. Plato believed in that platonic ideal, that somehow if one could distill the essence of something beyond its mere physicality we would encounter its perfect exemplar. Plato believed in the reality of ideas. For him, ideas actually exist—not physically, but they are real nonetheless. Physical objects, while necessarily imperfect, reflect, in whatever merit they may possess, the glory of the ideal.

From this viewpoint, the realm of spirit is actually *more* real, *more* worthy, than its imperfect, physical shadow. That notion—that to be physical is degraded; that somehow the spirit partakes of the universal while the body partakes only of the particular and, therefore, is inferior—is to be found not only in Western philosophy or in Eastern meditation, but in many Jewish articulations as well. From no less a guide than Maimonides we learn:

It was necessary that men's very noble form, which as we have explained is the image of God and God's likeness, should be bound to earthy, turbid, and dark matter. Which calls down upon man every imperfection and corruption; God granted it—I mean the human ideal—the soul, power, dominion, rule, and control over matter in order that it subjugated, quell its impulses, and bring it back.[2]

Make no mistake, Maimonides says, "You have the potential to greatness, your soul, which is incorporeal, knows only the Divine, but it is placed in a body which is turgid, and dark, and weak with all kinds of carnal desires. It is because of the flesh that you sin, it is because of the flesh that you err."[3]

As Rabbi Samson Raphael Hirsch, the nineteenth-century founder of modern Orthodoxy, writes to his nephew: "Respect your own body as the receptacle, messenger, and instrument of the spirit."[4] For him, at best, the body is a useful tool to be subjugated, dominated, controlled, but never trusted and rarely celebrated.

Before I critique this spirit-body split, I want to point out three important and valuable insights that we derive from this approach:

- Thanks to this split of spirit-idea and body-physicality, Judaism has, throughout the ages, always placed high value on ideas, on the life of the mind. Judaism has linked the spiritual enterprise with that of intellectual rigor. This has been a crowning glory of Jewish civilization and one that we ought to continue to celebrate.

- Because this view tends to assess what is important as the ideal, even when it is not the actual example that exists in a world, this is an approach that is very rarely compelled to compromise standards merely because a particular habit is the way it's always been. Plato and Maimonides will be the first to tell you, the way it has always been is degraded and inferior because it is compromised by physicality. It can always be improved.

There is a tremendous optimism to this view of striving toward an elevated ideal.

- This is a view that understands God as being ultimately transcendent, meaning God is beyond all physical limitations, beyond all human conceptualizations. The greatness of God looms large for those thinkers who live with the chasm between the body and the soul. For these thinkers, then, there is a built-in resistance to claiming to have complete knowledge of God or to be able to definitively speak on God's behalf. God's perfection is beyond all human assertion or articulation. This recognition ought to be a goad toward humility and making room for pluralism.

The Drawbacks of the Dichotomy

Despite these three considerable affirmations that a mind-body split makes possible, ultimately this dichotomy exacts more costs than it confers benefits.

The first drawback of this mind-body split is that if the ideal is only located in the universal, then every particular example is automatically inferior, implying that your deficit is located precisely where you are uniquely different from all other people. Someone who loves technology more than the average is a nerd; someone who is physically demonstrative is a fruitcake, and so on. Distinction is automatically viewed with suspicion or derision. A view that elevates the ideal is profoundly mistrustful of any individuality, of people being stubbornly not the ideal, of being irreducibly unique and different. It is also important to point out that if the ideal is perfect and if the physical is denigrated, then how much more so are people who are physically disabled or socially degraded: how inferior are they! It is easy with the split between body and spirit to create a hierarchy of the more spiritual (elevated) and also a hierarchy of the bodies that best approach the (spiritual) ideal. Those people count more than others.

I believe that splitting body and soul into separate camps also ultimately trivializes issues of social justice: don't worry that there are people starving because, after all, this world is already a degraded place and we need to focus on what is spiritually pure. How petty politics becomes when you are promised an eternal life with no corporeality whatsoever.

Finally, understanding God's perfection to be of another world, this mundane and ephemeral world need not occupy much of our attention. Even though we are melting the ice caps and incinerating the ozone layer, and species are becoming extinct at an alarming rate, concerns are elsewhere. From the perspective of a physical-spiritual dichotomy, these unfortunate events constitute corporeal trivia. Focus instead on eternal salvation! The view that the physical is inferior ultimately contributes to ignoring that we live in a remarkable and beautiful world. Ignoring the laughter can be fatal.

Soulful Bodies and Embodied Souls

We need not be chained to this toxic split. Instead, let us heed a different consensus within Jewish tradition, revealed through the lenses of contemporary Process Theology. This robustly corporeal approach, from its inception long before Plato, advanced a different case for the spiritual life. Rather than understanding that there is conflict between body and soul or assuming that we can separate out the two, this stream of Jewish thought has always insisted that the spiritual manifests precisely through bodies, that people are not disembodied spirits but rather *bassar ve-dam*, flesh and blood, an inextricable fusion that constitutes God's crowning glory. These Sages, early anticipators of Process Theology, taught that body and soul are interlocking aspects of a fully mature human entity and that both of them are necessary vehicles for holiness and godliness in the world. As transcendent as aspects of God may be, much of God is also immanent. God is to be found in each and every flower, in every breath we take, in the people who are sitting next to us, and in a world that God has made for us. "The world laughs in flowers," says Ralph Waldo Emerson.

Let's think about some of the bounty of a spirituality that is embodied, unafraid of the fact that we are human beings who occupy a physical world in which good and evil, holiness and profanity work out their ongoing struggles. It is said in the Babylonian Talmud's Tractate Ta'anit 11b, "Rabbi Elazar said, a person should always see himself as if holiness resided within his intestines." Imagine how the world would be and how we would treat our bodies if God were encountered not only in immaculate cleanliness, but in the really earthy objects through which we live our lives. What if we trained ourselves to value the holiness of our intestines?

I note that often the scholars who separate spirit and body into an airtight dichotomy are men. Many men don't always realize that the real advances of life occur exactly in those messy spots that need to be wiped clean, in those soft bundles that need to be dried and kissed, caressed and held. Holiness—ask any mother (and a growing number of dads)—is packaged in squirming little bodies. It is precisely in the physicality of babies, in the love we have for each other, and in our embraces, that God is to be found.

Through the perspective of Process Theology, we learn to treat our bodies and each others' as the centers of holiness that they are. We are taught in the Babylonian Talmud's Tractate Eruvin 54a, "If your learning is arranged in all your 248 limbs, then it is secure. If not, it is not secure."

However much knowledge we have, our body also has an intuitive knowing of its own. If our conceptual knowledge never becomes embodied prehension, we don't truly possess it. Our body possesses tremendous wisdom, and the people who tell us to ignore our body's wisdom are telling us not to listen with that inner voice that is our truest counsel. But it is there! The still, small voice speaks, and training ourselves to hear what it is that our bodies are telling us is the essential component of learning within creation. The body has tremendous wisdom to heal and to nurture, if we would but teach ourselves to listen to the wisdom of our bodies.

Putting Our Soulful Bodies in Action

It is the crowning glory of the Torah, and of the Rabbis (who were not themselves students of Plato and therefore weren't really aware of his mind-body dichotomy), to focus Jewish life not in people thinking abstractly together but in doing deeds of loving-kindness and holiness. Once we've embraced the Process perspective and transcended the split that elevates soul and distinguishes it from the corporeal, our priorities shift: not disembodied values, but values affirmed in relationship to each other and creation. It is what we do in a world that presents the venue for God to enter the world. Suffering is not an interesting theological problem; it is a call to action. Do you know people who are hurting? Help them. Do you know people who are lonely? Befriend them. Some of these deeds of embodied goodness are *mitzvot* and can be found in traditional lists of commandments. But many of them extend beyond any list of obligations and spring naturally from our connections to the world of which we are members and from our relationships to each other.

Because bodies are sacred and because the world is as physical and solid as it is, that physical presence is where God is best found.

Each moment offers us an opportunity for deeds of sanctity and holiness through which to transform that world into a place in which the love of its Creator is that much more apparent. The Babylonian Talmud's Tractate Yevamot 6b reminds us that "the Sabbath is an obligation of a body." Can we learn, finally, to see that the holiness of our bodies means that the holiness of other people's bodies is just as pressing an obligation? This means that performing acts of goodness for each other becomes a vessel for infusing the world with spirituality. Our ethical obligation starts with the searching eyes of other human beings. Our willingness to take their needs seriously is our willingness to let God in.

Please don't misunderstand me. I am not claiming that the search for interior spirituality is intrinsically bad. It need not be. There is much productive inner work to be done and much we have yet to learn from Maimonides, Plato, and others. But, in maintaining this dichotomy between body and soul in which bodies are fetid and souls are sublime, we obliterate the essential genius of Process Theology, inherent in much of Jewish tradition, which is to refuse to sever the two.

The Thresholds of Our Lives
Judaism's Rituals and
Observances of Becoming

In any human life, it is easy to move out of the moment and into a series of steady, small adjustments and modifications brought on by our aging, development, and passage through time. Instead of experiencing ourselves and others as objects—stable, constant, unitary, and substantial, as the dominant view posits—we are more like streams of flowing droplets—always on the move, never quite the same, shifting to match the world around us and the relationships in which we engage. We aren't solid and static. Rather, each individual is in process, always synthesizing and integrating new data into evolving patterns of personality, temperament, memory, and aspiration.

If Process Thought is teaching us anything, it is that we aren't human *beings*, so much as human *becomings*.

Just as Process affirms God meeting us in our concrete, specific reality at each moment with what we as entities face at that moment, so at every key moment of our lives Judaism offers specific rituals and observances that we optimally embrace to lighten our burden and sharpen our vision. In moments of transition, in places neither inside nor out—in such times and places Process allows us to make visible precisely how Judaism blossoms into ritual. The Process approach nudges us forward through word, song, and deed—not as abstractions but as real individuals, not in some timeless realm, but in the key moments of our lives.

Scholars call these occasions *liminal*, a term from the Latin for "threshold." To be liminal is to be aware of standing on the threshold of two different existential planes, on the transition point between two different stages or spheres. Take, for instance, the key celebrations and observances of the Jewish home. On the doorpost and between every room we are traditionally commanded to place a *mezuzah*, a ritual object of Torah that makes emotionally safe the transition between inside and outside, between one room and the next. In the doorway, one is neither in nor out. That is liminality, and Judaism offers the added measure of comfort, belonging, and meaning at precisely such indeterminate and ambiguous spots.

Liminality pertains not only to space, but to time as well. As we move through the day, Judaism offers moments of mindfulness as opportunities for formal prayer and unscripted reflection: *Shacharit* in the morning, *Minchah* as morning shifts to afternoon, and *Ma'ariv* as day becomes night. Each morning as we move from the relative unconsciousness of sleep to the awareness of waking, many of us mark the liminality of our minds with *tefillin* ("phylacteries" or boxes containing scriptural passages), *tallit* (prayer shawl), hand washing, and other rituals. Judaism walks us through these periods of greater flux and blurred boundaries, which are opportunities for new perspectives and fresh insight.

Sacred, Alluring, and Dangerous

Life is an open process, a series of events, as our growing from one stage of life to another moves us to a liminal phase in which our identities are not self-evident. Just as life is a series of self-surpassing possibilities, our expectations of behavior open up to new levels, and previous elements of self now give way before unheralded possibility. These moments of transition are enticing, holding out as they do the opportunity for novelty, achievement, and delight, which a Process perspective makes explicit. So, for example, a *brit milah* welcoming a baby boy opens to a dipolar analysis: a celebration of life and a recognition of new vulnerability on the part of the parents. Seeing our families as dynamic loci of becoming, we can acknowledge that the arrival of this new baby changes the identity of every member of the family and community, because we are all becoming-in-relationship. That new relationship renews each of us in unique ways. Those transitions are also terrifying, with an undercurrent of danger, uncontainability, and unpredictability. Small wonder, then, that precisely those moments attract religious attention and ritual—both to maximize their promise and to contain their threat.

- **Birth:** The first and biggest life transition is from nonlife to life. The gradual growth of a being from nonbeing, as the mother experiences the reality of new life within, grows in relationship with this promise of a future, and births this baby into a waiting world. *Aggadah* (Jewish storytelling) attaches the hope that each new child might actually be the long-awaited Messiah. *Halakhah* (the traditional Jewish way of living) offers the structure of *brit milah* (circumcision) for boys and *simhat bat* (rejoicing in the daughter) for girls as a way of expressing, containing, and celebrating this momentous eruption into life.

- **Adolescence:** The next major transition after birth is the period when one is no longer a child but not yet completely an adult. This period of adolescence is one of exploration, boundary pushing, anger, frustration, joy, and discovery, both for the adolescent and for the teen's family. Not yet capable of bearing the full burden of adult responsibility, yet chafing under the restrictions of adult supervision, this is a time of constantly renegotiated privilege and limits. No small wonder that Judaism launches this phase with a great celebration—Bar Mitzvah for boys, Bat Mitzvah for girls—helping all involved, and the community as a whole, to muster the love and caring necessary to sustain each other during this time of change.

- **Adulthood:** At this stage, the primary life tasks are meaningful work (compensated or volunteer, but a way of contributing value and meaning to the broader community), meaningful family (marriage and children), and meaningful community. Traditional Judaism doesn't have a ritual for launching a career per se, but it does provide a lyrical celebration of marital love. Standing under a wedding canopy, the loving couple reenacts the idyllic past of the Garden of Eden, anticipates the messianic redemption, and recalls the return of the Jewish people to Jerusalem and to an age of world harmony and peace.

- **Death:** This final transition is the mirror image of birth, as the individual merges back into the larger cycles of cosmic belonging, entering eternity (what the Rabbis call *olam ha-ba*, the "world to come"). All human living is a journey toward this inevitable juncture, toward separating from loved ones and transitioning from active participant to loving memory. Jewish ritual clusters around three primary values: asserting the reality of this loss (and its finality); honoring the dignity of the deceased; and offering comfort, community, and connection to the surviving mourners.

Recentering Our Focus from Separate Lives to Expressions of Covenant

This understanding of the life cycle as marking the beginnings and endings of different stages of life for each individual Jew contrasts with the dominant cultural perception that life belongs to each solitary individual, that we make autonomous choices as discrete individuals, and that our living links us only externally with other objects—human or otherwise—in the world. As such, it is merely about the transitions that a single individual is experiencing at each of life's stages. Such a view of life is constricted, brutal, and isolating.

But in a keen reflection of Process Thought, Judaism offers a deeper, far more profoundly spiritual approach to life—one in which our principal life task is not to dominate the center of our own concern. Recognizing that what is closer appears to be larger (but isn't really!), Judaism reminds us that what appears to loom large is a distortion of a more inclusive, integrated perspective. We loom large in our own imagination and narrative, but only because it is ours. Life invites us to live fully—to risk a perspective that sees the cosmos as a dynamic, integrated whole. We are significant to the degree that we relate to it all, not because of our perceived centrality but because of our real and dynamic relating. In the words of the philosopher Hans Jonas:

> Life thus faces forward as well as outward; just as its Here extends into There, its Now extends into Not Yet, and life exists "beyond" its own immediacy in both horizons at once.[1]

Each life—and every life event—extends beyond itself, connecting to what came before and what will come afterward, to our own locality and to the cosmos as a whole. Putting God at the center is how Judaism seeks to correct the distortion of our own self-absorption. "Do God's will as though it were yours, so that God will do your will as though it were God's. Nullify your will for God's, that God may nullify the will of others for yours," teaches *Pirkei Avot* (Mishnah Avot 2:4). This shift of centrality is not about denigrating our uniqueness or worth (we each, after all, reflect *tzelem Elohim*, God's image). Rather, it is about deriving our value and contentment from our rootedness in relationship, in our connection with each other and with all of creation. God is the supremely relating one, and we derive our purpose and meaning in the context of that connection. The Copernican revolution opened great possibilities by making the earth peripheral and moving the sun to the center. The Torah revolution offers exactly the same liberating growth by giving priority to oneness, relation, and integration while marginalizing self-centeredness and self-concern.

Armed with this insight, we can now envision the life cycle not as stages in the life of each Jewish individual, but rather as the unfolding expression of the covenant at every moment of each person's life. It is not *our* life cycle we celebrate; it is the life of the covenant linking God with the Jewish people that is worthy of our attention and that justifies our celebration.

Viewed only materially, the value of life dissolves in its own finitude. We are merely a collection of elements organized to perceive ourselves and our own fragility. Our life is one of struggle and inevitable end. In such a schema, celebration is a momentary distraction from a grim and indifferent doom. Placing ourselves at the center is a prescription for depression or insanity.

But the celebration of real connection, embeddedness, and relationship—to all that is becoming and to the One who invites greater complexity, goodness, and experience—is indeed an engine of hope and purpose, an endless living process. Judaism labels that connecting, that relating, *brit* (covenant). It is made real through the study and implementation of Torah. In the words of Professor Charlotte Fonrobert, formerly on faculty at the Ziegler School of Rabbinic Studies, now at Stanford University:

> Embodied life, suspended between birth and death, between becoming and decaying, is not transcended and thus left behind, but on the contrary, it is, as it is, imbued and infused with a new script, the Torah, which regulates it, guides it, and hence enhances it."[2]

Revisiting the Life Cycle as a Process of Covenant

Let's revisit the stages of the life cycle, not through the prism of each Jew's individual life, but through the Process lens of covenant and connection:

- **Birth:** The covenant has the capacity to be self-renewing, to begin again. Each individual Jew is an opportunity to get it right, to launch afresh, to enter the world with wonder, new eyes, and a clean slate. Each Jewish baby is an embodiment of covenantal hope, of the audacity of a dream in the flesh. *Brit milah* and *simhat bat* are opportunities to dance the newest expression of covenant into the world, to hurdle the story of the ancient Hebrews that much further into the future.

- **Adolescence:** Surely the weakest link in the chain of continuity is that moment when children realize that the Judaism of their parents no longer dictates their way. Our children, emerging from the cocoon of childhood, stand in the blazing light of adulthood, deciding to fly with their own brilliant wings. Whether or not the Torah provides the wind is the fateful commitment of each adolescent, and the future of the Jewish people hinges on the treble chant of thirteen-year-olds. Bar and Bat Mitzvah are the public enactment of this fragile yet durable renewal.

- **Adulthood:** Not merely internal, the Jewish people live as a flesh-and-blood people in a rough-and-tumble world. Finding a way to shine light into the world, finding a way to nurture and cherish the next generation, remains the fundamental work of a covenanted community: rearing children *al pi darko*, on the path they should walk—a path of justice and love. The rituals of adulthood are all affirmations of these sacred commitments, confirmation that it does, indeed, take a *shtetl* to raise each other and each other's children.

- **Death:** Just as birth is the covenant's opportunity for renewal, death is the occasion for value and memory. As the frail, tired, and habituated move on, the covenant community has the opportunity to affirm that each person's worth is more than merely instrumental, that each Jew, each person, each living thing, expresses perpetual worth as a manifestation of God in the world. And each deceased person is eternally retained in God's mind. By escorting their remains with dignity, community, and tradition, we affirm our own place as honored, valued partners with God and with the people of Israel in the work of repairing the world.

Imbued and infused with Torah, with covenant, the life of a Jew is a manifestation of caring and service, of connection and nurturance, of becoming and belonging. Such an unfolding is surely worthy of celebration!

Imperatives of
a Loving Heart
Responding to Life's Lure
through Sacred Commandments

One of the stumbling blocks separating many contemporary people from a richer religious observance is the invisible and smothering worldview that lurks behind the sacred commandments, *mitzvot.* Orders barked by a Sovereign in the sky, literally dropped on us in the words of the Bible, may seem like a caricature of real spiritual depth and nuanced religion. But for countless faith-based people, that imposed creed conveys their sense of what they "should" believe and, for many nonbelievers, justifies why they don't. Between this hyper-literal notion of a tyrant who literally throws the book at us and, for nonbelievers, the alternative of a vast, meaningless universe, is a third option. Process Theology recognizes that the cosmos itself is dynamic and becoming, that we and the world are invited to greater engagement, relationship, compassion, and justice. In such a worldview, God is discovered as much within as without, permeating us and the cosmos and luring us to act on our love and to implement our optimal purpose.

Process theologian John Cobb describes this interplay from the Process perspective as follows: "God does not establish a set of objective laws and then leave it to individuals to obey or disobey.

The relation between God and humanity is far more intimate. God's call comes moment by moment, and the human response is constantly new."[1] Judaism's *mitzvot*, then, are the deeds that allow us to meet and respond: to the Divine and to each other through our behavior. The commandedness of the *mitzvot* comes from within— the imperatives that emerge from empathy, love, and belonging— and blossom into the sacred actions that can transform our world and bind our hearts.

Thought and Action: A Dynamic Process

It is customary to introduce the subject of *mitzvot*, literally "commandments" of Jewish observance, by noting that in Judaism the deed is central whereas theology remains secondary. Perhaps unique among the world's religions, historical Judaism stresses expression through a detailed regimen of behavior that shapes every aspect of our waking lives (it even specifies permissible body postures while asleep). How and what we eat, the frequency and content of prayer, business practice and communal policy, life cycle and special moments in the calendar, criminal and tort law—all these and more are defined, debated, and implemented as the very paradigm of Jewish spirituality. Vast rabbinic tractates seek precision when it comes to the path of mandated and prohibited behavior (*halakhah*), yet leave the narrative (*aggadah*) of our thoughts, stories, and values down-to-earth and diverse.

Much like the mind-body split we discussed earlier, many scholars have introduced Jewish observance in exactly that way: commandments are primary and important; thoughts are secondary, hence mythical and unconstrained. But our complicating challenge is that many *mitzvot* do pertain precisely to the realm of thought— proper belief, the very concept of idolatry, morality, and ethical ideals. The specific forms the *mitzvot* take are often extracted from the rich loam of *aggadah* from which *halakhah* grows; that is, the practices meant to recall and live the creation, the Exodus from Egypt, understandings of an afterlife, or to reflect kabbalistic theologies of God's diverse manifestations permeating the world.

Rather than trumpeting a false triumphalism or choosing sides in an unwinnable conflict—as though thought and deed could ever be completely separated—a fuller Process understanding of Judaism as a way of life invites us to recognize the dynamic, almost organic way that thought and deed interrelate in a confluence richer than either would be alone. Thought expresses itself in action, behavior refines and clarifies our belief, and an unending feedback loop keeps these two partners of Jewish vitality dancing with each other, each expressing and modifying itself in response to the pull of the other.

Living Jews (and Friends) Living Judaism

In fact, rather than distilling thought from action as two separate entities, it might be more accurate to recognize them as phases of an all-encompassing process, or as fluctuating emphases that reflect the short-term focus of the viewer at the moment. Just as light has wavelike properties for one looking for light waves, and particle-like properties for one seeking light particles, so too *mitzvot* well up from the fecund swirl of thought actions and of action thoughts, or what twentieth-century rabbi and Process-influenced philosopher Max Kadushin felicitously termed "value concepts." Here, again, we see the refraction of the key Process insight that body and soul are not separate. There is no inert matter; rather, there is pervasive panpsychism, meaning to exist is to possess some level of self-determination and agency, to experience, and to respond. This idea is reflected in the rabbinic praise "*Mechayei Kol Chai*, God who makes all things live," or in modern parlance, the "designer of a self-organizing process."[2]

Process Thought provides the needed perspective, insight, and vocabulary to make visible this integration of objective and subjective, of physical and mental, already permeating so much of biblical and rabbinic Judaism. As Process theologian Catherine Keller notes:

> The fluidity of an emergent universe is the process of a becoming world. For a theology of becoming/*genesis* matters to the

spirit. Spirit *matters*: it takes on flesh. It is not just a matter
of the single incarnation, but of an enfleshment always and
everywhere taking place, and always differently.[3]

That living quality found so clearly in Judaism is precisely the source
of its vitality and longevity. Rather than a system of distilled ideas
or a code of behavioral ideals, Jewish observance is living Jews living Judaism and interested non-Jews enriching their own path with
nuggets of Torah. Just as a vital organism uses its mind to situate
itself in the world, to assess danger and opportunity, Jewish thought
situates us in the cosmos, offering thought experiments that suggest
deeper connections to the Divine and to each other. Seeking Jews
(and sympathetic others) discipline their minds to think Torah. As
the cosmos is always dynamic and changing, so our thoughts must
also stay dynamic and flexible to integrate the best of our experience with the most expansive integrations of tomorrow. And just as
thought discovers itself by tracking the actions in which it becomes
visible, Jewish thought requires the implementation of *mitzvot* to
actualize Judaism's potential to inspire lives of goodness and holiness. Responding Jews (and engaged non-Jews) mold their actions to
do Torah. Torah's wisdom applies to any seeking person and every
community desiring connection.

So our first recognition is that there cannot be Judaism without
mitzvot, any more than there can be a brain without a body. Let there
be no further question of divorcing this Jewish practice from Jewish
thinking—a body without a brain is a monstrosity. How we understand *mitzvot* in general and each *mitzvah* in particular will have a
tremendous impact on our dedication to a life of commandments
and to the particular commandments our communities will value,
teach, and do. To cite Catherine Keller once more, "Perhaps it is a
matter of infusing the commandments within the atmosphere of
the Eros: 'Arise my love, and come away' is also an imperative—a
proposition.... After all, the ethics of 'should and should not' may also
encode, *should* also encode the divine lure."[4]

Torah in Action: *Mitzvot* and *Halakhah*

So it is true that *mitzvot* emerge as implementations of the divine lure and as manifestations of Jewish thinking, expressions of Torah consciousness in the details of behavior. It is further the case that many brilliant sages have productively used *mitzvot* as elements to fashion a systematic expression of Jewish symbolic thought. The ancient Rabbis read the sacrificial system of Leviticus as an elaborate metaphor for the inner work of repentance and rectification of wrongdoing. The great medieval Jewish philosopher Maimonides expounded on the biblical and rabbinic discussion of the skin disease *tzara'at* as a metaphor for slander and gossip, itself a category of *mitzvot* known as *l'shon hara*. Jewish theologian Franz Rosenzweig painted a picture of Judaism's *mitzvot* of the calendar and its holy days as an elaborate metaphor for the way Judaism sanctifies the present rather than aspires for a salvation at the end of days. These thinkers and others did not deny the tangible, behavioral aspects of *mitzvot*, but used them as opportunities to delve more deeply into a level of metaphor and symbol where the *mitzvot* display particularly rich meanings.

Yet for all its resonances as a concrete manifestation and an evocative set of building blocks for Jewish thought, there is a special relationship between *mitzvot*—the sacred deeds—and *halakhah*, which is often compared to a tree—living, luxuriant, and supple. *Mitzvot* are not random behaviors and they are not abstractions set into deed. For religious literalists and liberals alike, *mitzvot* are the fruit on the tree of *halakhah*, and *halakhah* is the systematic effort of the Rabbis to translate the Torah into action. In true Process form, they are dynamically interconnected.

Halakhah comes from the Hebrew root *H-L-KH*, meaning "to walk." The true meaning of the word *halakhah*, then, is the walking we do as Jews. That walking is not static, no distillation of abstract principles imposed for the sake of conformity. Walking is an activity that engages our entire body. It is somewhat unique and differentiated for each walking community or individual, even as there are also sweeping commonalities across communal lines. In much of Western parlance, translating *halakhah* as "law" has meant accepting a negative valence (law versus love, for instance), a notion of imposed authority opposed to freedom, a uniformity that stultifies individuality and diversity.

Halakhah is none of those things. On the contrary, a study of the history of *halakhah* shows that it reflects an ongoing effort to translate God's love and justice into the fabric of Jewish living. *Halakhah* invites the possibility to transcend our own self-centered focus and orient our lives to embrace service and integration, while offering a palette of practice that allows each individual to paint a life of color and clarity.

The Hebrew word corresponding to "law" is *din*. There are particular laws (*dinim*) and there are specific topics of law (*dinei mamonot*, for instance, are laws of finance). According to rabbinic teaching, one can—and, traditionally, should—strive to act beyond the limit of the law (*lifnim mishurat ha-din*). While it is also true that *halakhot* (plural) are indeed collections or lists of laws and that a *halakhah* may be a particular rule, "the *halakhah*" refers not to any particular law, but to the system with which such rules are generated. Surely the popular notion of law as rules is not quite what we are after here.

So why not just speak of *mitzvot* without reference to *halakhah* at all? There are indeed thoughtful and sensitive contemporary Jewish thinkers who advocate just that, and they speak of the wisdom of each particular *mitzvah* as sufficient to justify engagement. Some offer this *halakhah*-neutral approach to *mitzvot* as a teaching tool—take your first steps without worrying about the final goal. Otherwise, that final goal can feel so overwhelming one would never take the first step. Others advocate a *halakhah*-neutral life of *mitzvot* as less constraining, more inviting. However worthy those goals might be, on the whole a broad consensus within Judaism resists severance of these two notions. A robust sense of Judaism as a living organism requires a way for its component parts to connect in dynamic integration; the whole is greater than the sum of its parts. That integrated whole is precisely what *halakhah* offers us. Without a systemic commitment to contextualize *mitzvot* in the evolving conversation of the Rabbis across the generations, each *mitzvah* flourishes (or withers) in isolation and there is no sense of growth, direction, or advance. As the English poet Robert Browning put it, "One's reach must exceed one's grasp, else what's a heaven for?" As long as we are alive, we grow, flourish, change. Holding on to *halakhah* as a system—as a relational process—precludes turning any particular rule into an idol, prevents freezing the life out of the living covenant between God and the Jewish people. *Halakhah* as a system is how the Torah continues to integrate contemporary perspectives, converses with science, and heeds the voice of conscience. *Mitzvot* without *halakhah* are ends in themselves, perfect like a snowflake, and equally static, brittle, and isolated. Jewish life deserves more, and worthy Jewish living requires it, which is why all streams of Jewish life articulate distinctive and strong expressions of *mitzvot* and observance in their own ways.

Honestly, Can We Admit What We Believe?

Halakhah is the ancient tree—strong, broad-branched, with gnarled roots extending deep in the dark, rich soil. Each branch represents a developing Jewish community—the more recent the branch, the more recent the community. One way to understand a *mitzvah* is as a leaf—transitory, beautiful, and linked to the entire tree and every other leaf while still reflecting its own particularity.

Perhaps another approach might be to look at the word itself. In Hebrew, the word *mitzvah* means "command" (although "commandment" sounds classier). For most contemporary Orthodox Jews, that translation accurately carries their living nexus of belief and practice—God is Sovereign, issuing verbal orders that we are rewarded for observing and punished for violating. My hunch is that for many Jews in ages past, that articulation would have felt right— but not to every Jew, and not even the most famous! Listen to Rabbi Moses Maimonides, arguably the most famous Jew of the Middle Ages, reflect on the nature of the authority of *mitzvot*:

The happiness with which a person should rejoice in the fulfillment of the *mitzvot* and the love of God who commanded
them is a great act of worship. Whoever holds himself back
from this rejoicing is worthy of retribution, as it states, ...
because you did not serve God with happiness and a glad heart
(Deuteronomy 28:47). (*Mishneh Torah*, Lulav 8:15)

Maimonides argues here that the motivation for observing *mitzvot*
should be joy at the opportunity to embody God's lure, delight
at being able to satisfy God's initial aim. A traditional medieval
commentator to his *Mishneh Torah* makes that insight even more
explicit: the commandments are compelling not because of coercion or authority, but because of their correspondence to goodness
and truth:

It is not fitting for a person to perform a *mitzvah* on the
grounds of obligation and compulsion, rather, as one who
is commanded and happy to comply. *One should do the good
because it is good, and choose truth because it is true,* thereby
minimizing the trouble involved in his mind. Understand
that it was for this that we were created, to serve our Creator.
When we do what we were created to do, we shall rejoice and
be glad. (Maggid Mishneh to Lulav 8:15; emphasis mine)

Despite the testimony of these and other medieval sages, my hunch is
that most contemporary Jews also think they are supposed to believe
in that dominating, coercive nexus (Sovereign/verbal orders/reward
and punishment), but don't. Many continue to try to persuade themselves that they accept it, but this despotic brew of imposed belief
abandons them in times of need and betrays them in times of cri-
sis. When a loved one falls ill, they are reduced to a choice between
blaming the victim for her own illness or having to pretend it is
for the best, despite the evidence (and her emotions) to the contrary. If you are one of those people, I want to throw you a lifeline:
while the Hebrew word *mitzvah* does literally mean "command,"

the Aramaic—the language of the Talmud and the *Kaddish* prayer—word for *mitzvah*, *tzavta*, means "connection" or "link." While most contemporary Jews don't believe in a God who verbally issues commands, most do recognize that *mitzvot* connect them to the Divine. Most Jews today, when they light Shabbat candles, eat a kosher meal, contribute *tzedakah*, or feed the hungry celebrate that they are linking themselves to something beyond themselves—God, Jewish values, creation as a whole, holiness. This reflects the Process perspective on the individual and the community:

> People are designed for community, and their individual well-being is bound up with the well-being of their community. They are also individuals. Just as a person's psychic life is distinct from the totality of somatic events, so also it is distinct from the community of which it is a part. Although the community is constitutive of personal being, it is equally true that personal being is constitutive of community. People are neither isolated individuals nor mere parts of a greater whole. They are persons-in-community."[5]

So perhaps the barrier to a greater embrace of the wonder of *mitzvot* is the gap between our convictions and our language. What if we said what we truly believe, which actually makes sense of our patterns of practice? We affirm that *mitzvot* connect us to God; link us to Torah and the best of Jewish values; forge a relationship between our individual lives, families, and those of the Jewish people around the world and across the ages. We affirm that *halakhah* provides a system to integrate our newest insights and advancing knowledge into the scaffold of Torah and the cathedral of deeds that Judaism erects in God's praise and for human betterment.

Back to Commandments, This Time through Connection

Now that we've been truthful to ourselves and to God, admitting that the connection we feel is what makes *mitzvot* seem beautiful, worthy, and compelling, we are in a position to revisit commanded-ness one more time, but on our own terms.

Turns out that our problem may not be with being commanded after all, but with the kind of commanding we mean.

Remember that Sovereign in the sky, rewarding and punishing for what we do or don't do? Most Jews have found that notion of God to be both untrue and demeaning—to God's love and justice, and to our human dignity (itself a Jewish value). The distorting assumption we indulged was to assume that *commandment* had to mean something like the orders of a despot or tyrant. God's power is coercive in that model, and our service would be a form of slavery. We are right to reject that notion.

But Judaism doesn't limit its metaphors for God to that of Sovereign. Instead, the Torah and the Rabbis call God Parent, Teacher, Lover, Spouse, Covenant Partner, Redeemer, Fountain, and more. Think of the way the desires of a loved one are imperatives for you, not because you fear punishment but because you seek your loved one's happiness and want to show your love. A great teacher sees a student's true potential and mirrors that possibility so the student is inspired and confident and able to surpass herself. A loving parent persistently believes in a child until that child believes in herself and achieves her goals. Frankly, the great leaders of Israel (one thinks of King David in his early reign) weren't imperious tyrants from afar. David was the father of his people.

Mitzvot are commandments, but not the way edicts are, not like bossy impositions of power. *Mitzvot* are commandments the way wanting to please your parent or spouse is a commandment. The way living up to your mentor's hopes for you is an imperative. The way delighting a child you adore is something you can't stop doing. *Mitzvot* are commandments because we are loved with an everlasting love and because we are inspired to yearn for God's intimacy and illumination. Love creates imperatives that ripple out from the core of our loving hearts, which is precisely where God abides. Love obligates from the inside, as caring and nurturing warm from within.

In that way—and only in that way—*mitzvot* remain what they have always been: commandments of love; trusted pathways connecting the Jewish people and much of humanity with the God of Israel; beacons lighting lives of justice, compassion, and holiness in a world too often cruel and harsh. They offer occasions of timely meaning linking us to our contemporaries, and linking one generation to the others in the process of revelation, in a grand affirmation of the possibilities actualized through lives well lived.

Revelation and a Living Relationship of Love

An Open-Ended Torah and Building Holy Community

Many museums display medieval illustrations of Moses receiving the Torah. The artists portray an arm descending from the sky holding a book, while Moses stands on the top of the mountain, reaching up—straining to grab the book that is handed to him. That illustration is, I think, an accurate pictorial presentation of the dominant view of revelation as shaped by much of medieval philosophy—eternal God, static immaculate Torah, passive (although worthy) recipient. But if you have made it this far, and if you can entertain a notion of God and cosmos as becoming, of the universe as relationship-in-process, then I invite you to recognize revelation as also ongoing, relational, dynamic, and continuous. Such a Process idea enhances our ability to participate in revelation.

Revelation: God and Human Co-creators

As we discussed earlier, the idea that revelation is a sacred relationship should not come as a surprise to those who are familiar with the Bible, Rabbinics, and Kabbalah, because we find that that same openness permeates Jewish tradition, which speaks of *matan Torah*, the giving of Torah, and also of *kabbalat Torah*, the receiving of

Torah—both active aspects of a dynamic relationship. Far from being relegated to the distant past, to a single day and a particular mountain, Sinai and revelation refer to a quality of relationship that is always and everywhere available: *"On this day they came to the wilderness of Sinai* (Exodus 19:1)—Every day that you study Torah, say: 'It is as if I received it this very day from Sinai'"* (Tanhuma, Yitro 7). Not only does this continuous revelation apply to the study of Torah (the book), but any fruitful teaching by any sage enjoys the status of Torah: "Everything that a diligent student will teach in the distant future has already been proclaimed on Mount Sinai."[1]

This open-ended Torah harvests a living, growing process, a pulsing relationship of love. No mere abstraction or desiccated set of rules, Torah takes concrete form in the specific people through whom it emerges into the light of day. God's presence is manifest in their specific language, idiom, bodies, and culture. Moving backward through time, we can trace this insight back across the ages:

- "The word of God can be uttered only by human mouths."[2]
- "Likewise with all the prophets and those possessed of the Holy Spirit: the supernal voice and speech vested itself in their actual voice and speech."[3]
- "The Shekhinah speaks from the throat of Moses."[4]
- "It is clear that [while God's precepts are given] through words uttered in Torah, they are also given through words uttered by elders and sages."[5]

As the Torah becomes real through the active participation of its human co-creators, the apparent conflict between the Documentary Hypothesis—the process through which God and the scribes, prophets, and Sages of Israel produced the Torah we now possess—and the veneration of Torah as the manifestation of the Divine in words finds resolution. Since the Torah represents the response of the Jews to a heightened experience of God—an openness to the divine lure—it is patently impossible and fruitless to argue about whether the Torah is divine *or* human. In good dipolar fashion, it is inseparably both. God "speaks" in, with, and through *us.*

An Invitation versus a Mandate

Recognizing Torah as a divine-human partnership means that the authority of the Torah is no longer misperceived as coercive. Like God, Torah's authority is persuasive: an invitation to wisdom, rather than an intimidation through fear. Jewish tradition labels that fear of consequences the "inferior *yirah*" (fear, awe, reverence). But the "superior *yirah*" is marvel or wonder. It reflects reverent awe at the staggering grandeur of cosmos, consciousness, and life! Such *yirah* responds willingly to persuasive, not coercive, power. This inviting lure is found, among other citations, in the book of Deuteronomy, when we are instructed to keep the *mitzvot* and observe them, "for this is your wisdom and your understanding in the sight of nations, who when they hear of these statutes will say, 'Surely this great nation is a wise and discerning people'" (Shabbat 88a). As we recognize the shift in the authority of Torah from corrosive coercion imposed to an offer of a wisdom that bubbles up, the Torah attracts attention and elicits observance because it is wise and beautiful and because it augments life. Obedience is no longer the fearful attempt to avoid punishment, but the free embrace of life-sustaining, self-surpassing wisdom.

In fact, the Rabbis make the same point in a wonderful ancient midrash. Recall how, when the Jews are gathered at the foot of Mount Sinai, the Torah describes them as standing as *betahtit ha-har*, "under the mountain" (Exodus 19:17). The Rabbis understand that curious phrase to mean that God "covered them with the mountain as a vat. God said to them, 'If you accept the Torah, fine. But if not, your burial will be here'" (Shabbat 88a).

But you cannot force someone to agree with you through coercion, even if you are God! So if Sinai is a coercive imposition, then the Jews are technically free of the obligations of the covenant. Astonishingly, the answer the Talmud records is that *we are not obligated by Sinai!* Jews are obligated to the Torah because of an event during the lifetimes of Mordecai and Esther. When they wrote and disseminated the teachings of the tradition, the book of Esther records of the Jews, *kiymu v'kiblu*, "They established and they accepted it" (Esther 9:27). As the Talmud notes, "They established that which they already had accepted" (Shabbat 88a). It is only because they freely accepted the Torah, because they responded to the divine lure freely offered and freely accepted, that the covenant linking God and the Jewish people was affirmed. God's initial aim—to propose a way of living that the nations will recognize as wise—flowed into the subjective aim of the Jews' response, "We will observe and we will hear" (Exodus 24:7). That relationship precludes coercion. Covenant thrives on invitation, a mutual yearning.

Choosing, Chosenness, and Holy Community

Such covenantal love elevates the place of ethics, and it means that morality becomes the capstone of religious Jewish life. But this has been true from the beginning. Think of the Torah as a mountain: Genesis and Deuteronomy, the base; Exodus and Numbers, the second level; and Leviticus, the peak. The religious core of Leviticus, the source that organized and gave the book its final form, is the Holiness Code, which takes its name from *Parashat Kedoshim*. *Kedoshim* details how to participate in holy community. The peak of Sinai, it turns out, is ethics, as the prophets themselves also emphasize. In Jewish religious understanding, ritual matters because it generates ethical seriousness; it creates a pedagogy of goodness and an agenda of grateful inclusion.[6] Our beliefs enter life through our deeds: "What short text is there upon which all the essential principles of the Torah depend? 'In all your ways, acknowledge God' (Proverbs 3:6)" (Berakhot 63a).

In the dominant theology with its either/or dichotomies, either the Jews are chosen, hence superior, or all peoples are equal and none are chosen. If God is the active choosing partner, then Israel must be the passive recipient of God's choice. But Process Theology's dipolarity allows us to transcend these binary dichotomies. Israel is an active partner in the process of chosenness: "We do not know whether the Holy Blessing One chose Jacob or whether Jacob chose the Holy Blessing One."[7] Another midrash reiterates the reciprocity:

> As soon as the Holy Blessing One saw Israel's resolution, saw that they wished to accept the Torah with love and affection, with fear and reverence, with awe and trembling, God said: "I am the Holy One your God."[8]

Jews choose/are chosen to live Torah in the world, both to build communities of justice and inclusion and to model that it is possible to embody such a life. But other peoples choose/are chosen, too, in ways that match their particularity and distinctiveness. The Torah reminds us, "It was not because you are the most numerous of peoples that the Holy One set [God's] heart on you and chose you— indeed, you are the smallest of peoples" (Deuteronomy 7:7). To this cautionary note, the Rabbis add:

> Not because you are greater than other nations did I choose you, not because you obey My commandments more than the nations, for they follow My commandments even though they were not bidden to do it, and also magnify My name more than you, as it says, "From the rising of the sun even to its setting, My name is great among the nations." (Malachi 1:11)[9]

Jews choose/are chosen for Torah and *mitzvot*, although most emphatically not because of intrinsic superiority. Other peoples are chosen/choose their own paths to holiness and righteousness. This understanding comes not just from modern rabbis and theologians but also from the Torah and Rabbinics. The prophet Isaiah exults, "In that day, Israel shall be a third partner with Egypt and Assyria as a blessing on earth; for the Holy One of Hosts will bless them, saying, 'Blessed be My people Egypt, My handiwork Assyria, and My very own Israel'" (19:24). He also inquires, "Is it too light a thing that you should be My servant, to raise up the tribes of Jacob and to restore the preserved of Israel? I will give you as a light to the nations, that My salvation shall reach to the ends of the earth" (49:6).

Jews are God's servants both to return Israel to a covenantal life, but also as a light to the nations of the world. The prophet Amos reminds us that others have been chosen, too: "Are you not like the Ethiopians to me, O people of Israel? says the Holy One. Did I not bring up Israel from the land of Egypt, and the Philistines from Caphtor and the Syrians from Kir?" (9:7).

All peoples are God's people; all children are children of God. The Rabbis, as well, comment that we chose/were chosen not because we are greater, not because we are more observant, not because we glorify God's name more. We choose/are chosen because God is discerned in our relationship—to God, to each other, to God's creation—and that relationship is not abstract logic, it is a particular relationship involving a people, a place, a history, and a way. And relationship is always in process.

Everywhere I Go
Process Theology's Embrace
of Israel *and* Diaspora

Is it possible to maintain a special affection for one piece of land, but to remember in the process to love all lands? That simple question may well be the key to our capacity to get along: for Jews to experience a level of unity as *am echad,* a united people, and for all humans to expand their capacity to gain strength from diverse perspectives. We all suffer from those who confuse their own strong convictions with objective truth and who compound that error by conflating their sense of truth with an exclusive claim to it. To combat this pernicious manifestation of the dominant worldview is one of the abiding missions of Process Thought. With its built-in awareness of dipolar thought (that A and B can both reflect aspects of truth) and that all thought is an abstraction that is one step removed from actual reality, Process Thought respects multiple perspectives, conceding with intellectual humility that more than one perspective may offer value and insight.

There are those in the Jewish community who treat the world as if it were bifurcated into two mutually exclusive territories: you can either love Israel or love everywhere else instead. If you love Israel, then Israel has to be the exclusive focus of your allegiance and, in your view, the only real place toward which Jews should cultivate a deep commitment and loyalty. Everywhere else is happenstance, where Jews merely sojourn in the wanderings that ultimately ought to lead us back to Israel, our one true home. There are some Christians whose view of a Holy Land closely approximates this perspective, complete with the conviction that Jews will be ingathered back to their true homeland, Israel.

Then there is an equally strident cluster of people who claim just the opposite; who say, "No, here we are in the Diaspora, and we have been fashioning meaningful Jewish lives in the Diaspora for thousands of years. Israel is no different than the rest of the world, and therefore, our loyalty ought to be to all of us, everywhere, and we ought not to be looking toward Zion as either home or center." This view also finds its parallel among those Christians who refuse to concede any special link to the land where the prophets of Israel walked and taught.

The short argument I want to assert is that both of these positions, derived from the dominant substance of metaphysics, are sterile and bring on their own collapse. Process Thought insists that we cannot love the earth in abstraction; we cannot just be everywhere and nowhere in particular. Having an identity means cherishing what is distinctively ours; remembering where we come from, not simply as a memory of our distant past but in order to re-create and reformulate our present, cultivating the hopes of our open future. Our rootedness in the earth is grounding, and we Jews have been blessed to live pretty much everywhere. To treat our ubiquity as nothing more than fortuitous is to miss out on the blessing of the reality of our diverse lives. Yet to confuse the bounty of our living globally with a rejection of our yearning for Zion and the distinctive wonder of a revived Jewish state in our own age would be an error of historic proportions and a betrayal of millennia of Jewish aspiration.

To counter both of these simplistic distortions, let us examine a few selective texts to arrive at a more nuanced view. The challenge, of course, in Jewish life is that we have precluded precisely this discussion. The one topic contemporary Jews are uncomfortable discussing with each other is Israel, because whatever our feelings about Israel,

Zion, Israeli Arabs, Palestinians, or Diaspora, each of us feels like part of an oppressed minority within the Jewish world. So we watch our words and try to say as little as we can. We can no longer afford the silence or the evasion. For the sake of Zion and Zion's children, it is time to speak a fuller truth.

God Fills All the Earth

Let us start very close to the beginning, with God's words to Abraham, the father of Jews (spiritually and biologically), Christians (spiritually), and Muslims (spiritually and biologically):

> Raise your eyes and look out from where you are, to the north and south, to the east and west, for I give all the land that you see to you and your offspring forever.... Up, walk about the land, through its length and its breadth, for I give it to you. (Genesis 13:14–17)

Abraham is given this prophecy of Diaspora not as a curse but as a promise. These words are a demonstration of divine bounty and plenitude. The fact that we will wander to the corners of the earth is presented as a great opportunity, itself a source of blessing. Notice that the Jewish agenda starts with the particular (*your descendants*), but it quickly merges into the universal (*all the families of the earth*). Jews' blessing as a people is meaningful to the degree that the people of Israel engage with, and benefit, the rest of humanity. The Bible invites Abraham's children to live in such a way that the rest of humanity is motivated to bless them. Confounding any ethnic narcissism, our blessing comes from the peoples of the world, and we get to choose *how* to earn those blessings by the way we interact; by the way we engage with the larger world.

Notice that it is the peoples of the world who bless themselves by us; in a sense that is where we *all* derive our greatest blessings. The measure of our worth lies in how we treat not the people who are similar to us, but in how we reach out to the people who seem to be profoundly different. That boundary-crossing universal intent is the measure of our greatness (in fact, "boundary crossing" is the literal meaning of the biblical *ivri*, rendered in English as "Hebrew"). When we spread out over the entire planet, we may be tempted to interpret that dispersion exclusively as punishment and curse, but, at least in this verse to Abraham, God is saying, "Not so!" Our dispersion is actually the fulfillment of blessing and bounty, and an opportunity for greater service.

A similar sentiment is found in the stirring words of the prophet Jeremiah:

> Thus says the Holy One, the God of Israel, to a whole community that I exiled from Jerusalem to Babylon. Build houses and live in them, plant gardens and eat their fruit; take wives and beget sons and daughters; take wives for your sons and give your daughters husbands that they may bear sons and daughters. Multiply the earth. Do not decrease. And seek the welfare of the city to which I will exile you, and pray for the Holy One on its behalf, for in its prosperity, you shall prosper. (Jeremiah 29:4–7)

Jeremiah reminds us that our leaving Jerusalem was not voluntary, and we Jews certainly remember the coercion of that expulsion. Keenly aware of the involuntary nature of our exile, we continue to anticipate and yearn for Jerusalem. But look at what the prophet instructs his generation: if you live your lives only yearning for what you have lost, you will squander the fleeting time you have.

We all face this existential longing for "home." For example, I enjoyed my childhood and teen years in the beautiful city of San Francisco. Like any good San Franciscan in exile, I have spent my adult life yearning for the Bay Area and wondering how in the world I wound up in southern California. During one such moment of longing, my then-teenage son, Jacob, turned to me and said, "Abba, you don't miss San Francisco. You miss being a teenager in the '70s!" I think he's right. One can spend a whole life ignoring the blessing of today because we continue to wrap ourselves up in the memories of yesterday. Jeremiah advises the Jews of his time that the only way to live fully is to live in the present, to live where you are, to bless where you are. Our lives—personally and communally—are bound up with our locale. So we need to live locally, to care for our communities and the people who live in our neighborhoods, and the neighborhood next to our neighborhood, and the neighborhood next to that—our cities, our counties, our states or provinces. Jeremiah assures us that this integration and engagement will be the basis of our prosperity and our bounty. We must allow ourselves to be where we are, and in that place, we will be able to thrive.

Elsewhere Jeremiah augments this argument:

> If you remain in this land, I will build you and not overthrow,
> I will plant you, and not uproot; for I regret the punishment I
> have brought upon you. (Jeramiah 42:10)

The prophet presents these insights as God's. There are those who think that God's perfection means never changing, but that is not Jeremiah's idea of perfection. Jeremiah anticipates Process Theology when proclaiming that God's perfection is the ability to admit having made a mistake, and it is God's greatness to risk showing regret. God regrets the punishment. The second point to note is that here the exile is portrayed as a punishment to be suffered. There certainly is a lengthy strain in Jewish tradition, perhaps even a dominant strain, construing the exile as punishment. But even within the framework of exile as punishment, returning to Israel remains, for Jeremiah, a personal choice. God instructs us to care and provide for those people who can return to the Land of Israel and, for whatever reasons, choose not to; which is to say, where we live is a real choice—both options can express and implement profound Jewish values.

We find a similar positive assessment of exile in the words of the prophet Micah:

> *The remnant of Jacob shall be,*
> *In the midst of the many peoples,*
> *Like dew from the Holy One,*

Like droplets on grass—

Which do not look to any [person]

Nor place their hope in mortals. (Micah 5:6)

We are scattered like the dew in the morning, and like the dew, we are meant to sparkle like the droplets on the grass. In precisely such dewy sparkle, we are meant to glisten as the morning radiance of humanity. We are meant to inspire people with hope, possibility, and vision. That is our opportunity, and we accomplish our task by scattering everywhere. Gathering all those droplets of dew into one container— I know this from living in Los Angeles—produces a swimming pool (very nice, but not inspiring). For droplets of dew to attain significance, they have to be scattered. So too the Jewish people: we work our magic not just by being gathered in one locale, but by also dispersing, and participating fully in all the communities in which we dwell.

If I were to pick a prophetic sentence that has most revolutionized the world, this might well be it: "Great is the Holy One beyond the borders of Israel" (Malachi 1:5). In antiquity, everyone's god was a local god. Everyone's god dominated a geopolitical district, and that god's power extended to the boundary of the district, but not beyond. The notion that an abiding oneness, a pervasive holiness is accessible to all people in all times, in all places, without any exceptions—that no one matters more than anyone else, that no place is more significant than any other place, that we are all exactly God's children, as we are—that radical teaching is the prophet Malachi's innovative contribution. God is God, for everywhere and everyone.

We find that same insight magnificently expressed in the Midrash Tanhuma, a medieval rabbinic commentary:

God began to gather the body of Adam to the four corners of the world, so that the earth should not say, "The dust of your body does not come from me." So that if he was taken from the east and expires in the west, the western part of the earth should not say, "The dust of your body is not from me, so I am not accepting it." Therefore God took it from the four corners of the world, so wherever the human dies, the earth should accept him. (Pekudei 3)

In the fashioning of human bodies, God took earth from the four corners of the world so that wherever the human dies, the earth should accept the remains, so that everywhere is home, and any burial is a homecoming.

Let's step outside the normal parameters of religion for a moment and observe the world through the prism of science. Are the continents permanent? Perhaps on a human scale, but in geological or astronomical units of time they are not. The earth is churning and moving; the way the earth looks now is how it will look for the rest of our lifetimes, but geologically speaking, the earth is a viscous, roiling liquid, so what is now won't always be that way. The continents, oceans, and mountains swirl and rise and sink. This rabbinic midrash reflects the same reality that science does: we are all, literally, composed of the entire earth, indeed, of stardust from supernovae millions of light-years away. The components of our bones, the cells of our blood, the air that we breathe— all that was used by others before us, all of it derives from the entire globe and the most distant cosmos. There is no part of the earth to which we are strangers, no realm of the universe to which we are not kin.

Everywhere we are is home. Home is where our feet are. Home is where our loved ones dwell.

God Dwells in Zion

Home may be where we and where our loved ones live, but it is also true that for the Jewish people and for any of us who see ourselves in the Bible's vision, a part of our hearts turns toward Zion, an aspect of our yearning recalls the days of our people's youth, and a wave of our joy rejoices in the miracle of the democratic State of Israel today. To fully grasp Jewish wisdom, we must also affirm the privilege and challenge of Zion and Israel.

In the book of Deuteronomy, we are told of Israel's special appeal to God:

> It is a land which the Holy One your God looks after, on which the Holy One your God always keeps an eye, from year's beginning to year's end. (11:12)

Viewing life from a Process perspective, we do not necessarily take the Bible literally, but we do take the Bible seriously. These may not be God's words separate from us, because God is not separate from us or from the world. As we have noted, the words of the Bible are God's Word, bubbling up through us. We, too, have a hand in crafting the words into Word, distilling Word into actual words. The words of the Bible are as much an expression of our own self-understanding as they are a reflection of the Divine.

The Torah portrays God as embracing the Process duality that all the earth is precious, but the Land of Zion is home. There are, of course, problems in any literalist assertion, including that God objectively loves one particular land more than any other. But one need not succumb to literalism to affirm an intersubjective *experience* of God's reciprocal love for the Jewish people, a love that makes that land special *for God and us*. God's relationships with other peoples may also elevate other lands for those peoples, but our relationship to God makes this land distinct and particularly precious for us.

That covenantal evaluation of *Eretz Yisrael*, the Land of Israel, continues throughout rabbinic literature as well:

> Ten measures of wisdom descended to the world. The land of Israel took nine, and the entire world took one. (Kiddushin 49a)

Think of the strong personal connection that inspires such sentiment, claiming that Israel has nine-tenths of the world's wisdom!

Wisdom is the ability to distinguish between what matters and what is trivial. Wisdom is the ability to identify what is really important and what is marginal, the facility to modify our actions based on personal or communal experience. Recall Process Theology's identification of the divine lure with an optimal choice toward greater relationship, compassion, love, experience, and justice. Wisdom is not measured objectively; it reflects an intersubjective engagement. So too here: the sense of Israel's beauty and distinction is no mere objective fact, but rather the cornerstone of a living Jewish covenant that shapes our communal life and spiritual resilience across the ages. And it reverberates throughout other rabbinic claims:

> Ten measures of beauty descend into the world. Jerusalem
> took nine, and the entire world took one. (Kiddushin 49b)

Have you enjoyed the privilege of walking the streets of Jerusalem? Have you witnessed the late afternoons when the radiance of the slowly setting sun intensifies the colors of the Jerusalem sandstone? The chiseled stones reflect red and gold, ivory and brown, and the air swirls with the scent of pine and rosemary. Strolling Jerusalem's winding roads, the Jewish mind contemplates the remarkable men and women whose footsteps preceded us in that place, awestruck at how truly ancient it is, sanctified by our memories, our prophets, and our experiences of God.

Having such a moment, and encompassing the vista of Jerusalem, I too exult: my God, this *is* the most beautiful place in the world! Yet Jerusalem's beauty is not just the beauty accessible to the eyes. The beauty of Jerusalem is also an inner beauty—the beauty of promise and hope. Opening our eyes reveals one facet of the Holy City's beauty; closing our eyes divulges the hidden facets of its beauty.

> *You shall arise and ascend to the place that the Holy One, your*
> *God, will choose* (Deuteronomy 17:8). This teaches that the
> Holy Temple is higher than all the rest of the land of Israel,
> and that the land of Israel is higher than all the other lands.
> (Kiddushin 69a)

This talmudic passage is objectively false. The Temple Mount, Mount Zion, is not more elevated than all other lands. But when a traveler arrives in Israel and proceeds from the coastal plains toward Jerusalem, the pilgrim ascends. The drive on the modern freeways rises from the plains up into the Judean hills, culminating in the sweeping vista of Mount Zion and the entire city. That climactic event might well evoke a sense of being on top of the world, no mere geographical claim but a spiritual and topological exaltation!

"Dwelling in the Land of Israel is equivalent to all the other commandments of the Torah put together" (Sifrei Deuteronomy, Piska 80). The ancient Rabbis are not encouraging us to minimize the other commandments; they are not issuing criteria of significance for disparate aspects of Jewish life. Rather, they are saying that living in Israel allows us to give ourselves entirely to the practice at hand, the *mitzvah* of that particular instant. In this case, what they are saying is that every time you stand in Israel, you permit yourself a consciousness of all our traditions welling up from the inside. Living in the moment, in a particular *mitzvah* performed with complete focus, opens access to the flow of the deepest pools of Torah.

Rabbi Yochanan said, "Anyone who walks four cubits in the Land of Israel is assured of inhabiting the Coming World" (Midrash Mishlei, chapter 17).

Maimonides teaches that most of us think of the world to come as temporally subsequent, chronologically after the completion of our lifetime. But that perception is an error. The deeper reality, claims Maimonides, is that humans can access eternity any time we open our hearts to it. Anytime we feel the peace of eternity, we are already there.

If we walk the Land of Israel mindful of the promise, then we already taste eternity in the very walking, in the awareness itself. As a child I grew up in a nonobservant family. Consequently, I didn't possess a pair of *tefillin* (phylacteries, the black leather prayer boxes the Bible mandates for head and arm during prayer) and never even saw them used until I attended a traditional *minyan* at college.

During winter break, I shared that experience with my grandmother, and she went into her hall closet and emerged with a set of my great-grandfather's *tefillin*. I vividly remember the first time I took those *tefillin* with me to Jerusalem. I stood on the veranda of my room, greeting the morning sun as it rose over the walls of the Old City, bound head and arm in my great-grandfather's *tefillin*, thinking, "This is the taste of eternity. This is a moment expressing all of time." Eternity is not the place by itself; it is what we bring to the place. But the Land of Israel can open us to the presence of eternity by virtue of our shared *and* our private experiences there across the ages.

The Challenge and the Paradox

What follows are insights from the classical Rabbis that are not often cited today because they oppose powerful consensus or contemporary sentiment. It may be that our path, between the inviting and treacherous "Zion is everything" on the one hand and the equally alluring and dangerous "Diaspora is everything" on the other, may be navigated through these wise insights offering a *derekh ha-beinoni*, a middle path not frequently attained.

> In that spirit, let's inquire, along with the Talmud, "Is Babylonia most of the world?" (Eruvin 28a)

In the citation above, *Babylonia* represents all Jewish communities outside the Land of Israel; that is, the entire Diaspora. The question masks a protest: one community doesn't get to assume that its practice is universally decisive. The choice of Babylon is not fortuitous—even the most influential Diaspora community is still not normative for the entire (Jewish) world. That denigration of the Diaspora is hardly rare in contemporary Jewish rhetoric. But look at the next selection for a more surprising perspective: "Is Yehudah [Judea/Israel] most of the world?" (Kiddushin 6a). This asserts that Israel doesn't get to be determinative for everyone else, either.

Maybe our attempt to impose one single center is itself the problem. The talmudic Sages juxtapose these two criticisms (neither

Babylon nor Yehudah is most of the world!), underscoring their recognition of a profound human need to appreciate the Diaspora for what it contributes to Jewish life worldwide, just as we also need to appreciate Zion for its many contributions. Neither place is *the* center, neither of them is normative everywhere, and neither displaces or replaces the other. As we learn from Process Thought centrality, all claims of what is significant emerge in relationship.

The Talmud's third critical question may well be the most shocking: "Judah in addition to scripture?" (Kiddushin 6a). No *geographic* location can be central for the simple reason that home base is always, everywhere, Torah. Our truest home is found in the written record of the covenant linking God and the Jewish people. No land, however beloved or comfortable, can claim centrality against the claims of scripture.

That ancient rabbinic assertion of the centrality of scripture to Jewish life and allegiance finds curious echoes in the insights of Hans Jonas and Leo Strauss, two marginal modern Jewish thinkers—brilliant scholars whose works are rarely read in rabbinical schools (although they are starting to be read in at least one of them!).

Says Jonas, "Palestine is not a refuge from the vicissitudes of the Golah; it is the *avant-garde* of the Golah."[1] For Jonas, Diaspora is not a matter of geography; it is a matter of existential distance from life lived truly. In rabbinic parlance, one might say that we are no longer capable of observing God's will completely. Again, Jewish tradition provides a powerful image of such wholeheartedness: there was a time when we brought sacrifices willingly to God's Holy Temple in Zion, and we believed we were doing exactly what God wanted. But those days are over. The Temple has been destroyed, and many of our people have been scattered. So even in Jerusalem today, we continue to be in exile, says Jonas. Indeed, claims Jonas, the fragmented, assaulted, and elusive nature of *galut* (the exile) is intensified and anticipated by life in the Land of Israel.

That same sentiment is affirmed by Leo Strauss:

The establishment of the State of Israel is the most profound modification of the Galut which has occurred, but it is not the end of the Galut; in the religious sense, and perhaps not only in the religious sense; the State of Israel is part of the Galut.[2]

Expanding *Either/Or* to *Both/And* with Process Insights

Many caring Jews respond to claims like those made by Jonas and Strauss by feeling the need to rush to Israel's defense. Any claim that Israel hasn't ended the exile, that Israel is itself an expression and product of the Diaspora, is viewed as a betrayal at worst or as a matter of dangerous confusion at best. Such a response, while understandable emotionally as an expression of commitment to the Land of Israel and the importance of national self-direction for the Jewish people, falls prey to a reactive and rigid dualism that forecloses the substantive exchange of ideas that drives Jewish dynamism. Redefining Israel's continuing importance *and* the Diaspora's continuing vitality need not denigrate either center of Jewish living.

To transcend the imposition of either center as absolute, we must use the Process insight of dipolarity, moving beyond *either/or* to embrace a symbiotic *both/and*. Frankly, this challenge is bigger than the Jewish people alone. The need for certainty and a monopoly on truth plagues much of contemporary life. Humanity has become so polarized that we are no longer capable of sustaining civil conversations. We are unwilling to learn from people with whom we profoundly disagree. This rigidity is itself a foul harvest of an ideology of eternal, absolute Truth.

We need to muster the courage to transcend *either/or* and to embrace the heady virtue of dipolarity, gleaning value from more than one pole. The totality of each of our identities comprises more than a single characteristic. Each of us integrates different partial identities, and the only way to determine which single component is our real identity would be to amputate significant aspects of who we are. I am a Jew, an American, male, human, father, son, husband, and friend. All those attributes inform who I am, so the best way to know me is to multiply these complementary descriptions, add them to each other, producing a rounded, cumulative picture of the person I am.

This dipolar, relational approach sheds light on the fullness of individual personalities in all their distinctiveness, and it remains illuminating for groups, cultures, nations, and for our tradition as well. I believe that the Process tool of dipolarity can elevate us above the falsely dichotomous argument: either Israel or Diaspora. Neither of these extremes enhance our humanity, neither makes us wise or worthy. It is time for our communities to desist from such a pointless and false dichotomy.

A Process approach to Judaism brings together two apparently incompatible perspectives:

- We can affirm Jewish life as beautiful wherever Jews are found, to nurture Jews (and all peoples) where they are, as they are, and to help them maximize their engagement in Jewish life, their lives of Torah, their performance of *mitzvot*, the beauty and the holiness of their lives, everywhere they are. At the same time, we live in an age in which the Jewish people in the democracies of the world have also taken their places as full citizens. We are not in our nation by virtue of someone else's permission, not because someone else has allowed us to do that. We are no less American, no less German, French, Brazilian, or wherever we hail from, than the other citizens of our countries. We also have a God-given role in those countries to help bring the peoples of the world together in open conversation, in mutual liberation, and in active engagement. That also is the contemporary and sacred role of the Jewish people. Whether we see our paths as taking us to Haifa, Los Angeles, Tel Aviv, Toronto, Berlin, Nabagoya Hills, or Buenos Aires, wherever it takes us we can celebrate that path as legitimately our own, and we can expect our fellow Jews to celebrate with us.

- At the same time, those of us who are members of the Jewish people, because we have a stake in the unfolding of our ancient covenant with God, have a dual commitment to celebrate the miracle of being alive in a period in which there is a democratic Jewish state in our homeland and to encourage and support any Jews who feel themselves invited to return to Israel. We, and all people of goodwill, can support them in such an act of loyalty, passion, and hope: to be able to assert before the eyes of the world and all peoples, that the Jewish people have no less a right to national self-governance than any other peoples on the planet.

We must nurture each other and support each other *where* we live and *as* we live. We are all of us, in that sense, Zionists and all of us on the road to Jerusalem. At the same time, Jerusalem is wherever we are. So everywhere we go we are going closer to God: we are living lives of holiness and engagement, Torah and *mitzvot*, compassion, justice, and beauty.

The Process of
Offering Ourselves
What We Do When We Pray

Praying is nearly ubiquitous, almost a synonym for being human. Wherever people are found, there you will find someone reaching out to the Oneness, the Cosmos, the Divine, the Mystery. Through words, meditation, movement, offerings, renunciations, charity, good deeds, protest, dance, incense, and a host of other practices, human beings from remote antiquity to the present day have stretched to create connections beyond themselves to something all-embracing, to create a connection more liberating and fundamental.

Oftentimes, the act of prayer springs from a deeper source than any ideology can express. Despite our belief or lack of it, despite our skepticism and our desperation (or because of it), we cry out, we plead, we negotiate. Sometimes we are moved to tears by a joy so deep it almost hurts, and we blurt out thanks whether or not we think there is someone there to listen. There are moments of sitting still, when listening to the quiet beyond words roots us and allows us to gain reservoirs of trust and hope we had not previously been able to access. We encounter seasons of sorrow so enervating that we can only curl up in the dark and enter the pit. "From the depths I call You, Holy One!" (Psalm 130:1). Help, in such moments, is more embrace than action; simply feeling held in times of trauma is an answer.

Of course, after the moment has passed, the cry released, the thanks expressed, we are left to wonder: What was I doing? Was that prayer simply giving in to magical superstition? Indulging a nonsensical childish dream? Distilling overwhelming emotion into words so I could release it? Perhaps. But I can't help suspecting that our *acts* of praying outstrip our *understanding* of prayer, that our moments of sincere outpouring are more real than the ideas we filter those acts through. Our outmoded philosophies and metaphysics often complicate our praying and can make real prayer elusive. Process Theology comes to unblock our outpouring hearts by braiding our intuition, our knowledge of the world, and the images that allow us to relate to creation and our Creator into a single blazing torch, capable of illuminating the crevices of our hearts and the four corners of the world.

We Pray Better Than We Theologize

Most people pray with the hope or expectation that their prayers make a difference: that God desires our yearning, that our focus contributes to a different (and better) outcome. Often our prayers are formulated as requests, as though God needed a reminder or gentle persuasion to do the right thing. Or we grovel with words of mollification, as though we could forestall a punishment or entice a reward if we got the words right, felt bad enough, or crawled low enough to remain under the radar of God's notice.

Despite the diverse motives we bring to prayer, most people have been taught by dominant theology to think of God as unchanging (eternal), all-knowing (omniscient), and in complete control (omnipotent). If God is unchanging, that means God must remain unaffected by our prayers (theologians call that "impassible"). If God is all-knowing, then God knows what we're going to say before we say it, knows the situation we feel impelled to pray about, and knows the future before it becomes real in the present. If God is in complete control, then whatever will be will be, and God already knows whatever will be, whether or not we pray.

If the situation is already known and the outcome is already determined, then perhaps the only role left for prayer is to stroke God's apparently insatiable ego. We repeat, "You are great! You are great!" to try to appease divine narcissism. After all, our dominant theologies already precluded the possibility of God needing our prayers, changing because of prayer, or modifying the foreknown outcome because of us. The only remaining function of prayer seems to be abject fawning. Frankly, don't you often feel that sentiment is what most of the prayers in the prayer book express?

There is something undignified about the whole enterprise. And yet ...

As I said, real people pray as though God cares about us and our sentiments, as if our words have an impact, as if the dialogue is real and the relationship transformative and desired. Our hearts already intuit what the dominant theology obscures. Perhaps the problem, then, is not with our practice, but with our ideas. Perhaps *our* challenge in prayer is to articulate the conceptual frame that honors the urgings of our hearts and the yearnings of our souls.

Prayer in Process: Meeting in the Moment

Process Theology offers a different filter through which the reality of prayer attains unprecedented and vibrant clarity. Recall that the Process understanding is that God is the One who makes all relationship possible, the One who generates all the options the future offers and empowers each and every one of us, as we are, where we are, to take the optimal next step if we so choose. Process Theology understands God as being so personal that God meets each of us in our immediate, concrete particularity: who we are at this moment, what we need now to take that best next step forward. That means that at every instant, God knows us (and every event in creation) not theoretically, not in a timeless theoretical way, but as we actually are—each of us, all of us.

God not only knows us as we are, but empowers us and all creation to reach for the optimal next step available to us from where we are. Each of us is offered our own optimal next step, and each of us retains the freedom to embrace that lure or to reject it. No abstraction, that lure is tailored to our reality—our current context and our distinctive individuality. As theologian Marjorie Hewitt Suchocki says, "God works with the world as it is in order to bring it to where it can be."[1] Because God works with the world as it is, when we transform ourselves we transform the world by precisely that amount, giving God that much of an opening to work with us, through us, and for us.

What are we doing when we pray? At the simplest level, with spontaneous or wordless prayer, we recenter ourselves with God at the core. When I was a child, I used to run my magnet through the soil in an abandoned field near my home. The magnet would attract the iron filings in the earth, and those filings would align themselves with the magnet as it passed by. With God as our magnet, prayer allows us to orient ourselves around optimal love, justice, experience, and compassion. We elevate our own sense of what is possible, the significance of our choices, and our capacity to make a difference. Since God works with the world as it is, that new/renewed energy and determination is now available for God's wondrous work.

We don't turn to God as magician and rule breaker. God works with, in, and through creation as it is. God is persistently, tirelessly luring creation toward its optimal expression—greater love, greater justice, greater engagement. Rather than breaking the rules, praying opens us to renewed expression of that lure and fresh zeal for its fulfillment.

Prayer as Reminder, Prayer as Script

For many people, the only prayer they encounter is a communal activity that consists of liturgical reading from a book. Please rise. Please be seated. Please rise. Please be seated. Often the book is very old. For example, the *Siddur*, the Jewish prayer book, contains prayers that range in age from thousands to hundreds of years old. How does reading someone else's words open us to a more attentive responsiveness to God's lure? Wouldn't we commune better if we prayed spontaneously and from the heart?

Of course, there is much to be said for the spontaneous out-pouring of the heart. It is noteworthy that in Jewish tradition two of the earliest biblical examples of prayer are exactly that: the distraught mother Hagar, seeing her infant Ishmael about to die in the desert, calls out her sorrow to God, and God answers her not with a super-natural intervention but by opening her eyes to see a well of water that was there all along. In good Process form, the lure is the capac-ity to take Hagar from where she is to where she is capable of going. With no rule breaking of natural law, God offers a life-affirming embrace made possible through self-determination and resilient hope. The next great unscripted outpouring of the heart takes place centuries later in the sanctuary at Shilo, when the priest Eli observes Hannah silently imploring God for a son. Again, no supernatural rule-breaking intervention is necessary—the young wife succeeds in bearing a son, whom she dedicates to the service of God. That young man, Samuel, becomes the greatest of Israel's judges and one of its earliest prophets. In both cases, spontaneous prayer is honored, and in both cases the Bible portrays it not in the mouths of the powerful and the privileged, but in the earnest entreaties of vulnerable, righ-teous women.

But Process Theology makes it clear that the choice isn't lim-ited to the dichotomy of one or the other, either spontaneous out-pouring or scripted liturgy. Indeed, the weight of Jewish precedent affirms the symbiotic relationship between the two. We will be best prepared for the unscripted exclamation if we devote the discipline to regularly scheduled prayer. The resonance of that scripted com-munal recitation will be that much richer because of the trails blazed by unscripted moments of crying out in anguish, need, or gratitude.

Liturgical prayer, then, is like reading a script. A great actor will allow the script to provide the content and context for his own per-sonality as a character. The actor becomes the character portrayed in the script, feels the character's feelings, motivations, anxieties, and aspirations that shape the character's personality. So, too, the person at prayer becomes the righteous, questing soul portrayed in the prayer book. We make ourselves into vessels to be sculpted by the values, aspirations, and memories provided by the *Siddur*. In emptying ourselves to be so filled, we express ourselves not as discontinuous and solitary moderns, but as instantiations of *klal Yisrael*, children of Israel, at one with our Maker. For the duration of our praying, those words become our words; those sentiments become our yearning. We expand beyond the confines of our own limited lives, the constrictions of our own age and place, and enter into a flowing stream of ancient and timely tradition. Such praying can make us more than we are alone. We grow to include our people around the world and across the ages. Through that expansive sense of *Yisrael*, we take on concern for all humanity and serve as stewards for all creation.

Process Theology and Prayer of the Possible

When we pray for someone else—a form of intercessory prayer, a prayer for healing or for the diminution of pain—what are we doing? Particularly since we've abandoned the notion of God as magician and prayer as insurance policy, what does it mean for us to pray for someone's recovery?

We live in interdependent relationship to each other and the world around us. Process Thinking highlights the reality that we are not solid, solitary substances but rather relating patterns of energy that weave our interactions with each other into the very fabric of our becoming. The foods we eat and the music we dance to weave our neurons uniquely and constitute our muscle and bone, as do the people we love and the faces we learn to recognize. Each of us is a dynamic composite of everyone we've known, every place we've been, in expanding circles of family, community, species, and planet.

One thing prayer cannot do is to vanquish mortality. All things come into being, flourish, decline, and expire. All becomings end. To pray for health and intend that a person should not die, should never die, is vain prayer. It is not the way of the world. Indeed, prayer cannot eliminate illness. Woven into the fabric of life are the viruses and bacteria that share our bodies and form the communities that we are. They sustain us, and they feed on us, and the rhythm of life and dying includes copious expanses of sickness. To pray for the removal of all illness is to pray for delusion. That too is vain prayer.

Yet we persist.

Knowing that illness and death are part and parcel of the human condition, we feel the need to *do* something, to *speak* hope and determination in the face of our own and each other's suffering, to strengthen our connections and to affirm our shared becoming. God works in, with, and through us. As we lift up others in our prayer, we focus our attention and energy on them, offering God and the world this new level of focus as a tool for renewed connection and integration. The Hebrew world *davar* means both "deed" and "word," and the *davar* of prayer is a worded action and a doing speech. We put those word actions out into the world, hone our energies as tools for well-being and affirmed belonging. We elevate and focus our *kavanah,* our intention. Prayer gives God the gifts of our intention, our energy, our hope to use to create deeper human belonging, greater engagement, richer connection.

In such a world, prayer for healing is meeting in a depth more resonant and aware than our normal consciousness. Affirming that God knows each of us as we are, and that God eternally internalizes each instant as it becomes the present, the act of prayer is the *davar* (word/deed) of meeting each other in God, in strengthening the link that connects us to our loved ones, to those far away, to communities in trouble or danger. We focus the vibrations of our minds and hearts, and direct that intention to God and, through God, toward the resilient, vibrating patterns of energy that are our loved ones, the objects of our concern. We strengthen the us-ness of them. We raise to explicit consciousness the vague concern for the other, and we sharpen that concern into praise, petition, and empathy.

Perhaps such prayer can nudge the trajectory of a disease; the scientific studies of such matters remain ambivalent in their findings. Prayer can speak to the depths of the sick, the struggling, the sad, affirming that they are not alone, not abandoned, and making it possible for us to meet them in God and mobilize untapped resources on their behalf—their own, ours, and God's.

In such a living Process Theology of praying word/deeds, we not only offer our prayers as words and deeds, we become our prayers. *"V'ani tefillati,* I am my prayer" (Psalm 69:14).

God Is Becoming
Tragedy, Judaism, and Process

A few years ago, tragedy struck at the heart of the community of the Ziegler School of Rabbinic Studies at American Jewish University, where I am dean. Joel Shickman, a beloved student, husband, father, musician, and friend, was diagnosed with a serious illness. His struggle was valiant and the students, faculty, and staff rallied around him and his family, but he eventually succumbed to the relentlessness of the disease and died in the fall.

Following his death, several members of the community felt unable to comprehend how God could have let that happen. Some spoke of feeling betrayed or unable to pray. As my students sought to regain their faith in the wake of tragedy and to better understand the way the world unfolds, I turned to Process Thought to offer a haven for those needing consolation, and a light of honesty and truth so our healing would be real.

Suffering, God, and Our Roles in Becoming

Many of us perceive the world as a collection of things—mostly static, isolated objects that interact but remain separate. Being is the core of that ontology. With Process Theology, science joins faith to demonstrate that this perception is a distortion. The core of reality is not being, which is an intellectual abstraction, but becoming, which is the key characteristic of all, including God. The universe is a welter of endless change as we and all around us reach the present as a result of the choices we have made, the "choices" creation has made, and the God-infused lure toward innovation, creativity, and righteousness. Process thinker Charles Hartshorne referred to that fundamental reality not as ontology but as hyathology, from God's dynamic name revealed to Moses in Exodus 3:14: "I am becoming what I am becoming" (*"ehyeh asher ehyeh"*).

Human beings, indeed all creation, are the result of both God's own decision making and our own decision making as co-creators. God, in choosing to create, created us. That means that our independence is not illusory or ephemeral. We, along with all creation, have real agency, and the choices we make are truly untrammeled, unprogrammed, and unforeseen by God. God is vulnerable to surprise and disappointment, just as we are. The universe unfolds according to its own inner logic, based on the propensities of physics and the cosmos. God cannot—and does not—suspend them based on moral standards. As prominent American rabbi and best-selling author Rabbi Harold Kushner says, asking the universe to treat you better because you are moral is like expecting the bull not to charge because you are a vegetarian. God did irrevocable *tzimtzum* (withdrawal), creating the reality of our own autonomy and agency, along with all creation. In the words of Process thinker John Cobb, "God has taken a great risk in bringing into being creatures with the amount of freedom human beings have. Sometimes one may wonder about the wisdom of that risk. A better response is to resolve that we will use God's gift in a more worthy way."[1]

Many of us misunderstand the nature of divine "power" as coercive, as omnipotent, which, as we have learned, Process theologians regard as a philosophical mistake, a religious disaster, and a source of emotional and ethical torment. Thinking of God as having all the power leaves us rightly feeling betrayed and abandoned—"Was I not good enough for God to intervene?" It leaves theologians in the position of Job's friends, discounting our core ethical knowledge in an attempt to defend the indefensible. As Bildad, one of Job's "comforters" intoned:

> *If your sons sinned against God*
>
> *God dispatched them for their transgression.*
>
> *But if you seek God*
>
> *And supplicate El Shaddai,*
>
> *If you are blameless and upright,*
>
> *God will protect you. (Job 8:4–6)*

We know good and evil; we are infused with that awareness by God. Our friend dying young was indefensible, especially if God is omnipotent. Hiding behind "It's a mystery" or "We can't understand" or "It's all for the best" is worse than unsatisfying because it requires either blaming the victim (in this case, Joel and us) or denying our ethical compass.

The Lure of Choice and Connection

This awareness doesn't mean we abandon a conviction of a loving God, but rather it invites us to grow past an almighty one. If God has truly ceded to creation the ability to make choices, then God didn't kill Joel, and looking for God in special effects mistakes theater or science fiction for life. God is found not in the suspension of nature's propensities, but in the intrusion of novelty and surprise in normally established patterns, in the abiding nature of hope and the transforming power of love, a power that is persuasive, not coercive.

I saw God being very busy throughout Joel's struggle—in moments of laughter and song, in the strength of the relating that bound us all as a community and kept Joel feeling connected through his very last minutes, in the determination to be there with and for his family throughout and beyond the ordeal. I never expected God to guarantee an outcome or suspend reality. I did expect to find God in the steady constant lure toward good choices and responsibility. And that expectation God did not disappoint.

In Process Theology, God is the ultimate exemplar of process, of the focus on becoming rather than being. God absorbs and is affected by all that happens, by all our choices, by the ways that the world proceeds. When tragedy strikes, our sorrows are not lost; they permanently become part of the Divine. Our joys and our lives are not forgotten, but rather they are eternally and objectively real in the divine mind. In that way, I can affirm that Joel is not ended, although he is no longer visible to our eyes. He, too, is a process, and the process never ends.

Ever Dying, Never Dead
Finding Gifts in Our Mortality

I am not generally one to brag in public. But married for almost thirty years, I know many are astonished to learn that I can still fit into my wedding *kippah* (head covering) and, perhaps equally impressive, my wedding *kittel* (white robe), which still looks as good as it did the day I first wore it. I wear that *kittel* at the Seder for Passover and during services for Yom Kippur, a day on which we live as though we are angels. Yet there is one way in which that aspiration remains very much untrue: Angels, according to Jewish, Christian, and Muslim understanding, are of two varieties. Some angels come into existence when they are assigned a specific mission, and they cease to exist the moment that mission is fulfilled. Other angels exist eternally and never die. That immortality is not our biology—we are mortal. The *kittel* is not only a symbol of purity and joy, it is not only what I wore at my wedding, what I wear at every Passover Seder, what I have worn for ten years on the holy days, but it is also what my remains will be buried in. It is not coincidental that on Yom Kippur many Jews wear what will become their shrouds. On this holy day we are the walking dead.

Out with the Old, In with the New

On Yom Kippur we are like the dry bones of Ezekiel, knowing that we are frail and finite. It is as if we are given a reprieve. We may be dying, but we are not yet dead. In that sense, the Process philosopher Hans Jonas teaches that mortality is the gift the living give to the future. The wonder of life, awesome and terrible, is that it renews itself constantly, by sloughing off the old and embracing the new. Jonas calls that *natality*, the way life is renewed through the birth of new, young individuals and a series of new generations. Just as we thrill that babies, infants, and children refuse to do things the way they have always been done, bringing a relentless energy to their lives and to ours, so too we know that what is old breaks down and gives way before the young. Life, in this cascading process of endless renewal, splashes across the millennia toward greater diversity, experience, relationship, and connection.

Midway through the afternoon of Yom Kippur, the congregation directs itself to *Yizkor* (memorial prayers)—*Hazkarat Neshamot* (Recalling Souls)—prayers that provide an opportunity to focus on those who have gone before. But Jews do so not from some neutral place, as though we were looking at some other species. We are ourselves on the way to death. We humans live as dying creatures. We are aware, to a greater and lesser extent, of the inevitability of our own mortality. Sometimes we push it aside; sometimes it comes crashing in on us. But as we sit in our sanctuaries, the liturgy reminds us "who shall live and who shall die, who by water and who by fire." We recall over and again through the words of the *Machzor* that we have a limited number of times when we will gather together to recite those prayers. We are conscious that the clocks of our lives are ticking.

Organizing Priorities in Light of Mortality

Human beings, like all living creatures, are events. Moment by moment we shift and change and move with time. Created anew each moment, we have the capacity to extend our consciousness beyond the limits of our own life span and to modify our character and potential with each new moment. A Process understanding of Judaism helps to highlight that ancient reality and to use it for our good.

Awareness that we are dying should serve to focus our attention on living. It should make what is unimportant less important. We do not have time to waste: not on people we do not enjoy being with; not on activities that are not compelling, necessary, or worthy. Our time is brief. Because we all are under the same sentence, it ought to be easier to forgive each other. The one who has wronged us is not some all-powerful divinity who will outlast the ages, but, like each of us, a brief and ephemeral flash of life in a sea of roiling sameness. We ought to know that our identities are not simply that of solitary individual beings. We are part of something larger than ourselves. As Process Thinking affirms, all being is being-in-relationship. We Jews are this moment's embodiment of *Am Yisrael*—the Jewish people—which has lasted through the ages and, if we do our part now, will continue to span eternity. And *Am Yisrael* is itself in relationship, a component of that living organism called humanity, which itself is a component of the biosphere as a whole. Everything is a manifestation of becoming-in-relationship.

Consider an odd aspect of Jewish belief and eternity: we pray in the *Machzor* and elsewhere for the coming of the Messiah. We say the *Ani Ma'amin*—"I believe with perfect faith in the coming of the Messiah." Notice that the liturgy does not say, "I believe in the Messiah." This Jewish pledge of allegiance is not for belief in the Messiah (a being), but in the *coming* of the Messiah (a process). Here's the catch: a Messiah, to be coming, can never arrive. Once the Messiah arrives, the Messiah would no longer be coming. At that point one could no longer believe in the Messiah's coming. Jewish beliefs are abiding affirmations. God is always One, the Torah was given to Moses—these beliefs do not become false over time. So if we are to believe in the eternal *coming* of the Messiah, then the Messiah must be eternally *on the way*. Because we know that the Messiah is always on the way (hence, never arriving), our job is to prepare the world for the coming of the Messiah, doing what it takes to make the world that much more messianic. We must engage in acts of justice and compassion so that even though the arrival is never completed, the work of the Messiah is nonetheless advanced; that is, the world has greater justice, compassion, inclusion, and welcome.

A Messiah always on the way reminds us of our goals and aspirations, but it is up to us to work for justice.

The Value in Always Dying

We can affirm the same paradox about death: during your life you will never be dead. You will always be dying. But within life you are never dead. Perhaps for this reason, people cannot imagine the conditions of their own death. We can conjure up the process of dying, but when we imagine ourselves dead, we think of ourselves being immobile. We imagine having a mind, having a body, watching our body at our own funerals. But that is not being dead. That is being bored perhaps, maybe even napping, but not dead. We cannot imagine being dead because we are always on the way, always dying. We are, like the Messiah, always on the way, never arriving, always in process. That inescapable limit means that our dying is about living—with awareness, gratitude, and urgency. Dying is not something separate from the process of living. Our lives are a persistent training for death, just as our death wafts back to force us to value our lives.

At the hour of his death, the Baal Shem Tov, the founder of the Hasidic movement, turned to his students and said, "Now I finally know the purpose for which I was created." He was not encouraging morbidity, as if life's only significant moment were our deathbed scene. He was teaching that each and every moment counts. Nonetheless, it remains true that whenever I start reading a novel, I cheat: I flip to the end so I can read the last couple of pages first. I need to know how the story turns out so that I can better attend as it proceeds. In that light, the Baal Shem Tov suggests that only when we look back at the completion of our life will we really understand the meaning of everything that transpired previously. It means that we prepare for death by living well, in accordance with God's and the Torah's values, and our own integrity—by living fully in each and every moment.

Presence but Not Present

In Tractate Megillah 15a, the Talmud teaches, "A righteous person who dies is only lost for the generation in which he lived." The Sages compare death to a person who possesses but then loses a pearl. That pearl remains a pearl even though it is no longer accessible to its owner. So it is with those who have gone before us. We do not have access to their physical presence, but is it possible to say that they are still with us? Don't you know from your own life, from the people who have touched your life and then have passed on, how valuable and how important their presence remains every day? As a Process concept, Alfred Whitehead termed this abiding impact *objective immortality*[1] or *permanent significance for the Universe.*[2] It means you know what your grandparents, parents, or mentors would have said at every given moment to anything you experienced, to anything you say or do. Their reality is like the pearl. They are not physically accessible to us, but they are very much present in our lives. As we remember their love, goodness, and giving, our memories fortify us for the ongoing task of living. We remember their best attributes, and we remember that time is fleeting.

Acknowledging and Appreciating the Process of Time

The Baal Shem Tov, again as he was dying, turned to God and said, "I hereby pledge a gift to you of the remaining hours of my life." The Koretzer Rebbe, one of his students, taught that this was a true act of *Kiddush Ha-Shem* (martyrdom). But we do not have to wait until our deathbeds to offer up the gift of our remaining time. It is never given to us to know whether we have several hours, weeks, months, or years. But imagine how elevated our lives could be were we to pledge:

> This time is no longer my time. It is my gift to God. And I will live my life in such a way that every moment is my gift to God. The way I treat the people I love and those I do

not love, I will offer up as a gift. The way I work to build community, I offer, God, this gift to you. The way I work to strengthen Judaism and the Jewish people, a sense of the family of humanity, the way I represent my love for Israel and for Zion—everywhere I do these, God, I give to you. The way I care for your creation and walk lightly on your beautiful blue-green planet, this God, I give to you, as a gift. My remaining hours, I give to you.

There is a blessing recorded in Pesikta Rabbati, a midrashic anthology approximately about fifteen hundred years old. It offers words to recite when visiting a cemetery, upon seeing the graves:

Blessed is the One who created you in judgment, who brought death to you in judgment, and who will raise you up in judgment.[3]

I would ground that ancient blessing with the following addition: God's love shines in judgment to create us—finite and precious—aware at each moment that our time is limited, that we will each join our mothers and fathers who have gone the way of all earth, that we are eternally dying and learning thereby to live.

Untrammeled Future
Freedom and Becoming

Process Thinking asserts that every creature has its own self-agency. All of us, from the smallest particles to human beings, have an appropriate capacity to make choices that shape our futures. Our decisions have an impact not only on ourselves: because our choices initiate certain actions while precluding others, those same choices impact the choices of other creatures, other events. For the Process thinker, then, the future is not known by any creature or even by God. It has yet to be determined. And our freedom (that is, self-determination) is constrained by our choices before the present moment and the sum total of the choices of every other creature or event in the cosmos. How we respond to that harvest from the past and where we take it is very much ours to decide.

In thinking about how I might help frame the issue of being alive as a matter of self-determination, I thought naturally of Milk Bones. Milk Bones, for those who do not live with spoiled dogs, are the boxes of little dog bonbons that we purchase to lavish upon our pets. But I want to tell you not about new Milk Bones per se; I want tell you a story about very *old* Milk Bones. It's a story about freedom.

When I was a kid I lived with a dog called Oliver. Oliver was named after the title character in the musical *Oliver!* back in the '60s. Some of you will remember that the actor who portrayed the Dickensian orphan had a haircut like the early Beatles style. It was a moptop, which was more or less what the dog sported as well. So even though she was a *she,* she was stuck with the name Oliver her entire life. Oliver was very much a house dog, and she used to go into every room where we were and follow us throughout the house. But every evening when we would put her to bed, we would take her downstairs and open the back door to the kitchen, which led to a stone basement—dark and cold. That's where she had to sleep (I don't know why my parents made that decision), and the only way we could get her there was to take a Milk Bone and throw it down the steps into the abyss. At that point we would watch Oliver wrestle with her doggy soul. She would rock back and forth on the top of the steps until in a single instant her doggy nature would take over, and she would run down the stairs. At that point we closed the door. We did this every single night for seventeen years!

What Is the Meaning of Freedom?

As a student of philosophy, I wonder in what sense can we speak of Oliver as free. After all, nobody coerced the dog's choice. She was allowed to do what she chose to do. It's just that her nature was rigged in such a way that, given that scenario, a hundred times out of a hundred, she would most likely act the same way. That insight, concerning her propensity to certain habits, causes me to wonder how different she was from us humans. How often do we tell ourselves, "Okay, this time I'm not going to do that," only to enter that scenario and find ourselves doing exactly what we had told ourselves this time we're not going to do? How many times have we broken the promise that we made to ourselves when our parents were doing something distasteful to us, "Okay, when I grow up I'm not going to say *that,*" only to discover our father's or our mother's spirit controlling our voice as we tell our kids *exactly* what we had promised never to repeat?

We all wrestle with what it means to be free. We wonder to what extent we are the captains of our own souls. To what extent are we, instead, the sum total of all the choices that were made for us or upon us—our instincts, our nature, our history, and our parents? To what extent is our freedom illusory? To what extent is it simply our pretending, something that is not authentically us?

The Captivity of Natural Propensities

There are several possible ways to understand freedom in the world. The first of them is a kind of determinism, the notion that everything that has existed will always exist. Whatever exists is the sum total of the propensities of physics, and they are, the scientists tell us, without exception. You can be an atheist or a theist in this metaphysics. But if you believe that the universe is the sum total of what is out there materially, and you believe that the patterns of physics can account for all of reality, that everything that exists is a motion of atoms and molecules that come together in a certain way that is rigidly determined by the practices of nature (or the determinations of God, if you will), then there are no real choices; everything is the effect of prior causes. As human beings, we are simply determined by our biology, our neurology. Our thoughts are epiphenomena of our nervous system, so we do what we do because we must—because that expresses our biology, because it manifests our genetics. In turn, our genetics is simply the application of our biochemistry, which expresses our chemistry, which manifests our physics. Everything is determined, inevitable, unalterable.

In such a worldview, everything is predetermined and nothing is free. There are great theologians, philosophers, and scientists who have affirmed that determinism is true, and there are great atheists, among them Baruch Benedictus Spinoza, who said that everything is simply the working out of natural law, and therefore everything is as we knew it must be. In this deterministic outlook, provided with enough information, one could, in theory, predict everything that was going to happen because every event is merely the working out of mathematical probability. As shocking as it may sound, dominant views in many religions often contribute to that deterministic view. Consider, for a moment, the following question: If God can foretell the future absolutely, if an all-knowing God means that everything that will be is already known by God, who stands outside of time, then what possibility remains for free will? Western religion, the way it is understood by the dominant theology (of omniscience, coercive omnipotence, and God's simple eternity), forces us to choose between God's all-knowing power and our apparent freedom. In the history of philosophy and physics, human freedom does not fare so well.

The very philosophers who make the argument that all is predetermined act as though the choices they make bear significance. The same physicists who insist that we are nothing more than particles working out trajectories delight in making new discoveries and advancing their learning. They cannot possibly believe in the coercive determinism they verbalize. They live as though free to decide their own futures, offering yet another instance where life as lived exceeds even the conceptualizing of some of our greatest scholars.

The Freedom in Divine Persuasion

Process Theology insists that the future is open before us. Constrained by physical reality and our own prior choices, we still retain considerable self-determination (as does everything in existence) to shape a future that is largely open to multiple possibilities. Strikingly, much of Judaism—despite the dominant theology—makes that same assertion.

But I want to hold out to you a very different vision of Judaism that shines through the prism of Process Thought in the contemporary period. The remarkable thing about our universe is that it is constructed on fixed natural propensities and yet it continues to produce unprecedented innovations. The universe keeps spawning new forms of being that have never previously existed. Evolution, in that sense, is a scandal. Put in place a bunch of fixed, inflexible, unchanging rules and out of that unfaltering regularity galaxies are spun, and planets, solar systems, and universes are created. On some of those planets—this one in particular—life! And life does not just continue

to replicate itself. Even though the mechanisms for life are fairly sta-
tionary, life generates ever new forms of being, new forms of living.

God makes novelty possible. Innovation and novelty are the
consistent suggestions of God at a cellular level, at a preconscious
level, that allow for creativity and change. It is God's persuasive—not
coercive—power that makes possible the recognition that tomorrow
does not have to be the mere recapitulation of yesterday, that we are
capable of shaping our future in new ways. Unique among all religious traditions in the world, Judaism portrays God in the Talmud
not only as a teacher, but also as a student. God is not a dictator who
imposes edicts; God is the great pedagogue. The Babylonian Talmud
(Avodah Zara 3b) says that God spends the day studying scripture,
dispensing mercy, and nourishing the world. A God who learns is
a God who teaches, and a God who teaches is not coercive. That
God invites us to make good decisions, to perceive right from wrong
because of what we intuit inside, because of the messages that God
constantly allows to spill out of our hearts and minds when we align
ourselves with God's initial aims. My favorite medieval rabbi, Rav
Saadia Gaon (ninth-century Baghdad) teaches in his *Sefer Emunot ve-
De'ot*, "The Blessed Creator does not allow [God's] power to interfere
in the least with the actions of people, nor does God compel them to
be either obedient or disobedient."

That message of radical freedom is what life is all about.
Judaism is predicated on human freedom. Our ability to do *teshuvah*,
to repent, would make no sense whatsoever if we were programmed
like robots. If we were simply told what it is we were to do and then
we did it without free will, there would be no occasion to repent.
We would either be perfect and do what the program instructs, or
someone would take us out and rewire us. Human beings are not
machines. We make free choices because freedom is built into the
fabric of life, hence, of Judaism. The Mishnah (Avot 3:15) teaches
us, in the words of Rabbi Akiva, "Everything is foreseen, yet freedom
of choice is given." Rabbi Akiva is telling us that our choices are our
own. One only gives *mitzvot*—commandments—to creatures capable

of choosing to disobey them. God tells us in advance, you can choose to deny what I ask you to do; that is in your power. Liberated from Egypt (*mitzrayim*), we experience God as the one who set free those who were slaves. God is explicit so that we do not misunderstand the implications of our freedom. God tells us through the book of Leviticus: "They are My servants, whom I've freed from the land of Egypt. They may not give themselves into any other servitude" (25:42). You may not indenture yourself to wealth, fame, prestige, social status, or habits. You have been set free.

The Bad and Good of Freedom

So with this information comes bad news and good news.

The bad news is that we are free. There is no one who will clean up after us. There is no one who will prevent us from hurting each other or being harmed by other people's bad choices. We are on our own. The world has been given to us, and it is ours to determine how it will fare. Kohelet Rabbah, an ancient midrash to the book of Ecclesiastes, tells a beautiful story about our responsibility and our freedom:

> When the Holy One created the first person, God took Adam and led him around all the trees in the Garden of Eden. Take a look at how beautiful are my works, how splendid they are! Everything that I made, I made for you. Take care not to despoil the world that I made for you, because if you do, there will be none after you to fix it. (7:13)

The bad news: we are free. We are responsible for our choices and our choices are untrammeled. Choose evil? You may. Choose sin? You may. Give in to your momentary impulses? You may. There are consequences to those choices, but the choices are ours to make.

The good news: we are free! We are capable of making good choices. We are capable of learning from the mistakes that we have made. We are not trapped by the decisions that were made for us or by us. We are not trapped by our genetics. We have been given the gift of freedom. The future is ours to make and that means there is an unprecedented tomorrow awaiting us. As Rabbi Abraham ibn Ezra writes in his commentary to the Torah (Exodus 21:6), "Going free is comparable to the renewal of the world." We are, all of us, capable of renewing the world.

Conclusion
Judaism—A Personal Affirmation

Judaism is a way of life, a philosophy, a discipline, and the cultural expression of the Jewish people throughout the ages. An embodiment of faithfulness and robust hope, Judaism encompasses the communal act of transforming Torah, the Five Books of Moses, from literature into lives well-lived. One of the world's oldest ways of being human, Judaism is at once a portal into a universal perspective on the cosmos, life, God, humanity, and justice, and a love affair with a particular people, otherwise obscure and small except for the spiritual light they shine on humanity out of all proportion to their numbers. These elements are burnished to a lustrous shine when illumined with the light of a Process perspective.

A Way of Life
Judaism is not a conglomeration of distilled ideas, but a spiritual-ethical discipline that retains the capacity to elevate consciousness, heighten compassion, and inspire righteousness. A pathway for living an abundant Jewish life is the observance of *mitzvot*, the sacred deeds of Jewish practice. Some Jews practice these more literally and others more metaphorically, some more strictly and others more existentially, but at the heart of all contemporary expressions of Judaism are the many ways Jews translate these imperatives in their lives and communities. These *mitzvot*—613 in the Torah—span the range of what some would label ritual, psychological, *and* ethical.

Mitzvot energize a Jew while waking in the morning. They guide a Jew throughout the day, mandating use of just weights, fair business practices, compassion for others, giving charity, offering words of greeting to strangers, engaging in honest relationships, practicing mindful eating, and avoiding gossip or malicious speech. They encourage us to recite prayers three times each day and even when we go to sleep, with particular blessings for the evening, including a prayer forgiving those who wronged us during the day and another asking guardian angels to surround us in our slumber.

Being a Jew means embracing the opportunity of the next *mitzvah*.

Being a seeking Jew means enacting religion with one's entire body; for some that includes wrapping oneself in a *tallit* and *tefillin*; for men, being circumcised; for many women, monthly ritual immersion; and on and on. Judaism is the diversity of what different Jews do, creating a fusion of body, heart, mind, and emotion into a single unity that is greater than any of its parts. That unity is a Jew. That dynamic harmony is Judaism.

Judaism is a way of life not only for each individual, but for the community as a whole. Every occasion of the life cycle is a celebration of the *brit* (covenant) embracing God and *Am Yisrael* (the Jewish people), birth and *brit milah* (for boys) or *simhat bat* (for girls), commencing young adulthood as a bar mitzvah or bat mitzvah, marriage, illness, and death are all contextualized as expressions of the life of the Jewish people as a whole, an event of significance for our ancient covenant. Even the cycle of days, months, and years are illumined by the prism of the Jewish calendar. Shabbat (the Sabbath) sanctifies the seventh day each week as a day of rest and renewal, and the sequence of Jewish holy days and festivals mark the seasons and moments in the cosmos and the relationship between God and Israel that continue to frame our connection to the present.

These strings of sacred deeds are given coherence and life by a process known as *halakhah*, which literally means "walking," or the way. Often translated as "law," it is far different than some brittle set of rules or a nitpicking obsession with detail. *Halakhah*, the way, is communal choreography—Jews dancing across the generations and around the globe. Our *halakhah* roots us in the ways our ancestors and Sages have worked Torah in every aspect of our lives, communal and individual. By molding our behavior to express Torah, we Jews take on the role of God's hands, reaching out to bring healing to the world, and inspiring gratitude that allows us all to breathe in the giftedness of life and to share it with each other.

Halakhah, the way, begins in study. Those born into Judaism start their study at an early age, and those who choose Judaism engage in a lengthy study process prior to conversion. Historically, we read the Torah three times a week, completing the full reading each calendar year. We study the Mishnah, Talmud, and codes of law that began in antiquity and continue to this very day to trace how others before us have brought God's presence into the rhythms and practices of their waking moments and communal observance. Contemporary sages continue to apply *halakhah* to new situations, either unprecedented novelty or circumstances made new by fresh insights and ethical advancement. *Halakhah*, like the process that is Torah, is alive and continues to produce new branches, new foliage. It remains, as it has been called for centuries, an *etz hayyim*, a tree of life.

A Philosophy

Like any way of life, Judaism surfaces in the deeds and actions of Jewish bodies, it breathes an *embodied* way of life. Like all embodiments, it dynamically expresses and generates ideas that can only be fully experienced in the doing. This "knowing" bubbles up from our experiences, an almost intuitive harvest from our doing: *hitbonenut* in Hebrew. Process philosopher Alfred Whitehead called it *prehension*.

Those intuited ideas are not less important because they emerge from experience, but more so. At the heart of Jewish doing is the conviction that there is a unifying Oneness that undergirds everything and makes openness possible. That Oneness exceeds all human description or definition, but permeates all being and invites us continuously to surpass our previous limits. It is because of that Oneness that the cosmos is not a mechanical repetition of the same events endlessly, pointlessly. The cosmos blossoms into increasing complexity, connection, relationship, and consciousness because, Jews insist, the cosmos has been and still is beckoned toward greater becoming, greater liberation. We call that Oneness *God* and encounter the presence of the Ancient One in our holy deeds. We see the continuing lure, toward cosmos as the divine flowering of redemption. Through participation in creation, we connect to the Divine.

For Judaism, then, God is author of creation, an intuition that bids us to decipher the world's wonder in order to reveal aspects of its Maker, our Maker. For that reason, Judaism is enthusiastic about scientific research, both theoretical and practical. We welcome any new tools or insights that allow us to peek behind the curtain of superficiality to understand cosmos at a deeper level.

Another pathway toward the Divine is the texts of revelation. We perceive the Blessing One not only through the ongoing process of creation, but also, perhaps more intensely, through the distillation of human listening into words. Scripture—Hebrew scripture in particular—is an extraordinary cumulative process of engagement, as generation after generation of priest, prophet, and sage listened with an inner attentiveness and distilled divine bounty into words. Those words coalesced into stories and laws, compiled by disparate schools of ancient Israelites and woven together into a sturdy tapestry of Torah across millennia of collaborative effort. Jews believe that when we join in that process of attentive listening, straining to hear the Living Voice among the words of scripture and aided by the reverberations of our own attentive soul echoes, we too can harvest unprecedented Torah anew. We stand again at Sinai each time we draw new Torah into the world. In that sense, Torah is both a product (a collection of books) and a process (the act of distilling God's presence/will/invitation into words). Judaism uniquely portrays the Divine as a teacher, paradise as a school. Our continuing reading, learning, and commenting splash an ongoing cascade of Torah into the world, *mekor hayim*, a fountain of life.

We have been harvesting Torah from the moment of our birth as a nation. The great medieval sage Rabbi Saadia Gaon teaches that "the Jews are a people by virtue of Torah."[1] We tell the tale of our emergence as a people in response to the bounty of God's out-pouring, through the inspired gift of the prophetic insight of Moshe Rabbenu, Moses our teacher.

Our Teacher, Our Rabbi

Moses was great in a way that few are great. Having been raised among the abusive power and ostentatious wealth of Pharaoh, he nevertheless identified with outcast Hebrew slaves. Fleeing the deadening trap of court and caste, Moses found a freedom surpassing imagination in the wilderness, a voice calling him to mobilize the people for freedom. From the start, the Hebrew mind has heard the Compassionate in a call for human liberation, for justice and empathy. It was God working in, with, and through Moses who gave us hope that we might break the chains of generations of habit and hurt, who forced us to surpass ourselves and march into the unknown promise. It was God in, with, and through Moses who brought us to Mount Sinai and launched the process of Torah that has nourished us for the last three thousand years. That Torah—in a very real sense the Torah of Moses—powerfully locates the service of God in an expanding ethical circle, first a couple, then a family, then a tribe, then a people, then humanity, then a planet, finally a cosmos. God and Moses gave us the only real universalism, the kind that honors particularity and celebrates diversity. It was God working in, with, and through Moses who insisted that the fruit of faith is moral rigor, persistent love, and abiding justice: "You shall love your fellow as yourself" (Leviticus 19:18); "You shall love the stranger" (Deuteronomy 10:19); "You shall lift the burden with your neighbor" (Exodus 23:5).

Culture

Of course, no one can live forever at the base of a thundering mountain; nor can we remain on a peak in direct communion with the Sublime. At some point we all return to life as it is lived, to imperfect humanity and to flawed societies in need of our service, vision, and work. To survive in the world, an ancient way of life and philosophy must forge a way to thrive in reality, in the everyday. For Judaism, that mode of survival has been the cultures of Jewish people in every age.

Jews carried their Torah with them wherever they journeyed. First we wandered from Mount Sinai in the wilderness to Mount Zion in Jerusalem, there creating what the ancient historian Josephus called "one Temple for the one God." That Temple stood as a symbol of unity and uniqueness, the visible representation of the human aspiration to fulfill God's will perfectly and completely. It was an attempt to step, as it were, out of the messy welter of life. That Temple and its vision succumbed to human violence, jealousy, and conquest, assaulted by Assyrians, destroyed by Babylonians the first time and by Romans the second. In the wake of its destruction, the Jews discovered *galut* (exile), the wandering that means one is never fully at home, nowhere finally at rest. We learned that the pursuit of empire is a delusional security; the seeds of its own demise are sown in violence and reaped in blood.

As a result, we Jews are always on the way, always in process. There is no place to live in stasis, no way to be complete while we're alive. *Galut* is now a universal condition for everyone.

But we do not travel alone. Everywhere we go, we still bring our Torah with us. We live our *mitzvot* and whirl the ancient dance of *halakhah*—observance, study, commentary, life. Our ancient Torah has blossomed in ways we would never have expected: Jews learned from the cultures in which they lived and gave back—poetry, philosophy, and medicine with the Arabs; history, science, and commerce with the Europeans; film, journalism, humor, and scholarship with the Americans; art, literature, nationalism, drama, statecraft, and war with modernity. The range of Jewish culture is truly a microcosm of the world's influence, a gift of our hosts (willing and unwilling) to the evolving, conflicting meaning of what it is to be a Jew.

Today there are vibrant Jewish communities across Canada, Latin America, Europe, and even parts of Africa and Asia. There are two great centers of Jewish life: the Jewish people have returned to their homeland in *Eretz Yisrael*, the Land of Israel, to work toward forging a society of democratic values and the flourishing of a broadly Jewish culture. Through the autonomy and self-determination that a Jewish state makes possible, we are developing an equitable relationship with the other religious and ethnic groups within Israel and secure peaceful relations with Palestinian and other Middle Eastern neighbors. Jews everywhere find a part of their heart bound up in the State of Israel and its flourishing. Jewish communities in America are also exploring what it means to be full participants in a robust democracy, in which separation of religion and state creates the space for a rich religious diversity and a flourishing cultural identity. In both centers of contemporary Jewish life, questions of exercising power, ethics, inclusion, and justice in accord with the highest values of Judaism remain an ongoing challenge and opportunity. In both centers, deciphering how to be Jewish in a non-Jewish world remains challenging.

Faithfulness

Yet amid all that diversity, one simple standard remains: a Jew is someone who resonates personally with the history of the Jewish past and who identifies in aspiration with Judaism's destiny yet to be. We speak almost every language and look like all of humanity. We still read the ancient words of Torah in their original language, still pray to the same universal God our father Abraham encountered, still walk the way shown us by our rabbi, Moses. We still question and discuss, as we learned from the ancient rabbinic Sages of the Talmud, and we throw ourselves into social causes with the indefatigable desperation of a people who refuse to be taught to despair.

And yes, we are still occasionally "stiff-necked and stubborn," as Moses told us we were. Sometimes our stubbornness is for the good. We continue to hope.

We are an ancient people, ever young. We possess a wise and encompassing tradition, ever supple and open. Our mother city, Jerusalem, is the home of three monotheistic faiths, and our scriptures tell a tale of unearned love that resulted in creation, and a passion for justice that resulted in the liberation of slaves. We have been commanded to love and to liberate ever since. Many human liberation movements share our story—that of Moses and the Hebrew slaves—as their inspiration as well. Our story begins in the particular—a people wandering toward its land—and culminates in the universal—a day when God reigns supreme and all peoples find a home in our home, in which the Holy Temple, renewed symbol of a glorious human unity, is truly "a house of prayer for all peoples."

On that day, the world will know *shalom* (peace). We must join hands to make it so.

Epilogue
A Father's Letter to His Son

My Dearest Jacob,

As I write these words, you stand on the threshold of your birthday. For almost your entire life, you have struggled to forge a life of dignity and connection, despite the burden and stigma of autism. Your struggle has become our struggle—to provide you with the support and love you need to formulate your dreams in life and to reach for them, to help you live in community and contribute to its vitality.

I begin with that challenge because my journey is now inseparable from your life. In rabbinical school, any naive, superstitious faith I may have harbored was already seared under the light of the critical study of Bible and Rabbinics, the awareness that different clusters of ancient Israelite Sages and prophets gave words to our scripture and that those messages reflect the various perspectives of kings, priests, and prophets. Somehow we were supposed to absorb a natural history of the Bible's formulation and words, while still accepting God as the Sovereign whose will the Torah reflects. But I don't recall being told how to integrate those seeming disparities.

After ordination, as a congregational rabbi, I saw all kinds of life dramas: spousal and child abuse, drownings, illness and death, betrayal and distress. I also saw remarkable heroism, of the quiet everyday variety—love, loyalty, persistence, and refusing to surrender. When you and your sister were born, our blessing was so complete and, then, became so complex. Your diagnosis made it harder for me to clutch my liberal theology with a Monarch on high who might not manage every detail but who was nonetheless in control of the guaranteed outcome. As a diligent Conservative rabbi, I tried to help our community take on the *mitzvot* as God's commands and to see the Torah as the expression of God's will. But I lost hold of the rudder with your diagnosis.

For some time, I found myself lost and drifting. I still loved God and Torah, but I felt that there was a rift, that I could not stand with you and still mouth those sentiments about Sovereign and commands, reward and paradise. For quite some time, I said nothing. I would not be disloyal to what I knew or to whom I loved by failing to assert that you did nothing to deserve autism, that it was neither punishment nor judgment, that God is neither arbitrary nor cruel.

Your mother jokes that I started my doctorate to make sense of your autism, and I think there's a lot of truth there. I needed to think this reality through, to make sense of our life journey together. After all, I spent my professional life serving God and Torah, devoting myself to good deeds and acts of kindness. It wasn't supposed to happen to us.

I knew that the God I loved did not do this to you. I knew that God loves you as persistently and relentlessly as your mother and I do. But I didn't know how to articulate what I intuited. I didn't know how to think about it clearly. For me, liberal Jewish theology fails because it treats God's nature and actions like a sealed, impenetrable box. We know the input—science, philosophy, humanities, scripture, tradition—and we know the output—justice, compassion, *mitzvot*, love. But concerning what exactly God is doing and how exactly God is doing it, liberal theology has nothing to say, no specifics to offer. The Power that makes for salvation, the ontological presupposition, the irreducible triad with human and world, the partner in dialogue—these are all lovely images, but what is God actually doing? Right now, what is God doing?

While reading books of science and theology—about quantum uncertainty and relativity, of evolution and neurobiology, brains and minds and consciousness, I came into contact with a remarkable group of people who threw me a lifeline. I was able to build on the thoughts of many wise people—Henri Bergson, Alfred North Whitehead, William James, the Pragmatists, Teilhard de Chardin, Charles Hartshorne, John Cobb, and others—who insist on explicating what goes on inside the box, too. They talk about how God's love is reliable and persistent and irrepressible. How at each and every moment, God is giving us and all creation the capacity to rise to the right choice, is holding out that best possible choice to us, is granting us the ability to be self-transcending. God, according to the Process thinkers, is liberating love calling us to be our best possible selves. Just as God is self-surpassing, dynamic, and relational, so too—at our best—are we.

My new Process friends insist that God is not simply an impersonal Force (although God has Force-like manifestations), not simply a Power or a Ground of Being (although God manifests in those ways, too). They speak of God using biblical and rabbinic endearments: Father, Mother, Teacher, Lover, Spouse, Partner, Companion. Hearing them love God reminded me that I already knew those ways of loving God and that I first encountered them in the Torah's Hebrew and the Aramaic of the Talmud and Midrash.

Einstein's great revolution in physics emerged from one simple claim: that the speed of light is absolute for all frames of reference. With that one simple-sounding assertion, absolute time and space were revealed to be illusory approximations, and gravity was no longer a force—it was a response to presence. My Process friends helped me to name what I know: that God is not omnipotent, and with that claim, God's omnibenevolence shines strong: *ha-tov v'ha-meitov* in all frames of reference. Theodicy retreats as an intellectual puzzle and becomes what the prophets supposed it to be: a goad to action.

Partially, that is because chaos isn't something. It isn't a thing at all—it is absence, potentiality, no-thing. Call it *tohu va-vohu*, call it an eternal sea of quantum uncertainty; regardless, chaos does not raise the issue of dualism because it isn't anything—it is the lack of any existence whatsoever. All creation comes from God, who is the sole Creator. Whatever is created is created (and re-created) first by God and then by God in partnership with the creature itself, interacting with each creature and all of creation.

You see, Jacob, we are not static beings with some unchangeable core that bumps on the outside into other static solids along the way. From physics and Kabbalah and Torah, we learn that it all began as light and that we, too, are composed of packets of energy (light) slowed down to matter.

We, like the rest of the cosmos, are both process and event. We (and creation) are re-created each and every moment, integrating our most recent choice into our character, our history, our constraints. We are, at every moment, unique and self-surpassing—an event. We are, through each expansive re-creation, also continuously self-expressive in each new moment—a process. Perhaps that is why the Torah refers to our totality—body, memory, identity—as *nefesh* ("soul"). You don't *have nefesh;* you *are* one.

God's persistent inviting love lures us toward our best possible future. That choice, while free, is not random or directionless. Not all choices are equally godlike. God holds out to us that choice, which maximizes our relationship to each and all and expands our compassion, awareness, goodness, and joy. There are better choices and worse, there is righteousness and sin. God invites us toward *tzedek* (justice) and *chesed* (loving-kindness). But God leaves the decision to us. That means that the creation is not a one-time event; it is continuous and self-surpassing. It means that the giving of Torah is not an event in the past, but happens anytime we are open to receiving and harvesting Torah. This dynamism explains how it is that *halakhah* can originate in our covenant with God and is therefore dynamic and responsive to new information, new insights, new expressions of dignity and justice. How we determine to respond to our life is our decision and our task. Life is about learning to listen, reaching for hope, aiming high, and then daring to act.

It means that the future isn't merely a crapshoot. God has engaged in a *tzimtzum* that is real and irreversible. (One cannot consider creation to be real if its creations don't demonstrate the ability to relate, to choose, and to have an impact on each other and on the whole.) God's steady, persistent call is more powerful than any alternative. If we rise to our godlike possibility, then we muster a crucial role in bringing God's vision into reality. That is the teaching of Kabbalah and Hasidism, it is—I believe—the teaching of the Torah and prophets, and it is the teaching of Process Theology, too.

On a personal level, I believe that what the future entails is that we continue, as ourselves, beyond death. Our existence is real, and God knows everything possible to know and knows it eternally. That means that God knows us eternally—which is how I understand *hayyei ha-olam ha-ba*, life in the coming world. We exist continually in God (which turns out to be how we've always existed). My understanding of Process metaphysics affirms that, too.

For years, Jacob, I tried to mobilize people to take seriously the commandments of the Sovereign. Truth be told, it never worked very well. Few people thought that God actually spoke those words in the first place, and life was demanding enough as it was. Fear rarely motivates observance. But my Process friends help me find words for a deeper truth I already intuit—that effective commanding is an expression of love and is inspired by education, not by fear or by force. Jacob, I would do anything for you, for your sister, for your mother—not because I fear you but because I love you so much. If we are in covenant with God, then we recognize the *mitzvot* as compelling—not because of some external authority or threat, but because of the extent of the love, the marvel, the wonder of our finding ourselves alive in the cosmos, as Jews. The closer the relationship, the more compelling and numerous are the ways of enacting that intimacy. If we Jews seek closeness to God in covenant, small surprise that we count the ways of living the love in the hundreds of *mitzvot* that make our lives holy and link our way to those of our ancestors and the wisdom of our tradition. "God so loved Israel that God surrounded them with *mitzvot: tefillin* on their arms and heads, *tzitzit* on their garments, and a *mezuzah* on their doors" (Menahot 43b).

Far from becoming merely optional or folkways, the *mitzvot* in this understanding gain an irreplaceable urgency that embodies delight, companionship in times of joy and sorrow, at our waking, and throughout our days. Precisely because God's power is not coercive, we need not focus on resisting an imposition. God's power is persuasive, and the *mitzvot* are God's teaching tools for a life rich in perspective, resilience, and joy. Scripture speaks of a *kol d'mamah dakah*, a small, still voice. I think that's what Process thinkers mean by the lure. We sense that our intuition is God's lure when it is life-affirming, when it calls us to more empathic relating, more compassionate justice, solidarity expressed through engagement, more expansive love. If you ever find yourself summoned to be small or stingy, know that this voice is not God's, and try not to let it distract you.

My beloved son, what all this means is that your future is not fixed and you are not defined by your label. God works in/with/through you, so your decisions—day by day and step by step—can open up a future that you would never have thought possible, indeed, that previously wasn't possible. We've already seen how your steady determination to communicate and to control your behavior has led to your having mastered challenges beyond anyone's expectations.

We have seen that God's love is stronger than anything—not as something separate that beams down from above, but as a steady inspiring capability you have within, and which you also derive from the women and men who embody and convey God's love—people like Dr. Ricki Robinson and Darlene Hanson, like those teachers who believed in you and inspired you to rise to your highest potential; and above all, people like your Ema, whose love for you won't take "no" for an answer—not from the bureaucrats who wanted to put you on a shelf, not from the Jewish institutions that thought that showing us pity while treating you as invisible was the civilized option, not from the educators who pressed us to settle for "life skills" or the people who glared at us at parks, restaurants, airports, and pools for daring to live our lives in the light. Your mother, like my mother, too, models God's liberating, uncompromising, insistent love—the kind of love that brings Pharaohs down and liberates slaves. Small wonder that when I pray to God, I often use God's female names—*Rachamama* (a formally masculine word, to be sure, but one redolent of *rechem*, God's womblike qualities), *Shekhinah* (Abiding Presence), *Hokhmah* (Wisdom), *Binah* (Understanding). My friend Rabbi Judith Edelman-Green shared with me a new name for God, coined by Aya, one of her students with special needs in Israel. That child calls God "ElohEma" because God's love is like her mother's. There is wisdom in us all.

Some people consider this Process vision of God as weak or incapable. I've never understood the reason for discounting Process Theology on those grounds. I suspect that these critics want to believe in a Sovereign who controls everything (and will clean up after them), but don't really believe it. But the denigration is more mystifying to me because every time I've overcome a challenge I've faced, I've done so not because of some externally imposed mandate or fear of consequences, but because someone believed in me and showed me that I could do more than I thought I could. "Love is stronger than death," we are taught. Love is the strongest force in the cosmos.

So, Jacob, on your birthday, I want to remind you of what is already planted in your heart: God loves you with an everlasting love. You are not defined by your past or your labels; none of us are. You have everything you need. All you need to do is to listen with your heart, aided by the wisdom and energy contained in our sacred writings—the Torah, Talmud, Midrash, philosophy, poetry. As you attend to the still, small voice, refresh yourself in the cascading splash of generations of sages, prophets, and rabbis who have listened with their hearts and distilled God's love into a wise way of living large. If you follow your truest intuitions and our Torah's most all-encompassing teachings, God will be your renewing strength and your feet will be fleet like the deer.

On your birthday and always, my son, know that you are loved,
Abba

Acknowledgments

This book offers an overview of Process Theology from a Jewish perspective and looks at various aspects of religious life through the Process lens.

It began as a published symposium in the journal *Conservative Judaism* (volume 62, nos. 1–2 [Fall–Winter 2010–2011]). I cannot begin to express the extent of my gratitude to the chairman of the journal's editorial board, my colleague and friend Rabbi Dr. Martin S. Cohen, who painstakingly edited the special issue of *Conservative Judaism* in which the core of this collection first appeared. He has been a stalwart friend and mentor every step of the way, and I thank him for the gift of our friendship.

I am happy to thank the esteemed respondents to my original article: Jonathan Wittenberg, Catherine Keller, Harold M. Schulweis, Sandra B. Lubarsky, Rivon Krygier, Alfredo Borodowski, Michael Marmur, Michael Graetz, Tamar Elad-Appelbaum, David Ellenson, Lawrence Troster, and Norbert M. Samuelson. A subsequent issue included a response by Michael Knopf. Each of these fine thinkers crafted worthy and insightful essays, which I commend to you without reservation. We did not include them in this book only for the sake of streamlining the work and exposing the nuggets of Process Theology to a broader audience, but they remain well worth reading and I offer each of these authors my deepest gratitude.

I am also happy to thank the membership and leadership of the Rabbinical Assembly, the international association of Conservative/Masorti rabbis, of which it is my honor to be a member.

Thanks particularly to its president, Rabbi Gerald Skolnik, and to its executive vice president, Rabbi Julie Schonfeld, who have walked with me as partners as we seek to strengthen Jewish community and humanity with a love of God, Torah, and *mitzvot*. The Rabbinical Assembly was the publisher of the original journal, and is copublisher of this book, with Jewish Lights.

Having expanded the original journal article into this book, there are many people to thank:

Thanks to my friend Stuart M. Matlins, visionary founder, editor in chief, and publisher of Jewish Lights; Emily Wichland, editor extraordinaire; Kaitlin Johnstone, masterful editor and coach; Kelly O'Neill, skilled publicist; and the talented people at Jewish Lights, who accepted an unfinished manuscript and produced a beautiful and significantly better book.

While writing this book, it has been my delight to serve as the Abner and Roslyn Goldstein Dean of the Ziegler School of Rabbinic Studies and vice president of American Jewish University in Los Angeles, California. I am reminded daily of the blessing of working with an outstanding group of people: students, faculty, administration, and lay leaders. My deepest thanks go to the university's president, Dr. Robert Wexler, who is both mentor and friend; to Rabbi Cheryl Peretz, Rabbi Aaron Alexander, and Reb Mimi Feigelson— partners in building a world-class rabbinical school in the context of holiness, goodness, and friendship; to Rabbi Adam Greenwald, partner in creating a preeminent center of Jewish outreach; to the superb members of the faculty; and to my beloved students—rabbis and soon-to-be rabbis. It is a privilege and a joy to work at such a wonderful *makom Torah*.

My continuing thanks and affection also go to The Jewish Theological Seminary, where I was ordained as a rabbi and where I still cherish friendships and many close ties, and to Hebrew Union College–Jewish Institute of Religion, where I was granted the privilege of doctoral studies under the scholarly and humane supervision of my teacher and friend Rabbi David Ellenson.

I do not want to miss this opportunity to thank the extraordinary souls who form the heart of Process Theology, a true community of caring souls who transcend geography, confessional, and professional boundaries to embody the very relatedness they preach and explore: my newest rebbe, Dr. John Cobb, for providing insight and inspiration; colleagues and teachers, Professors Philip Clayton, Roland Faber, David Griffin, Catherine Keller, Sandra Lubarsky, Jay McDaniel, C. Robert Mesle, Thomas Oord, John Quiring, and John Sweeney. You have given me a fellowship of caring, shared curiosity and passion, and welcomed me among you. I am grateful and delighted to stand with you.

Of course, my beloved family has provided a constant backdrop of love and support. I am deeply grateful to my mother, Barbara Friedman Artson, and her companion, Richard Lichtman; my father, David Artson, and his wife, Jeanne; my sister and sister-in-law, Tracy and Dawn Osterweil-Artson; my niece Sydney, and my nephew Benjamin; my brother Matthew Artson; my brother and sister-in-law, Danny and Shirli Shavit, and our nephews and niece Alon, Roy, and Maya; and Grace Mayeda, my beloved childhood nanny.

I have been privileged to have many wonderful rabbis and spiritual guides enrich my life—too many to list—and I am grateful to each and every one of them.

My children, Jacob and Shira, fill my life with profound joy and purpose. They have both shared and shaped the Process, and I would not be who I am had it not been for their persistent love and lure. The rewards of seeing them grow into such kind, compassionate, and decent people is purest delight. Jacob and I have had many Process conversations, and he and Shira both exemplify the process of making good choices in order to be self-surpassing and to help heal the world. To see them emerging into their own fills me with joy and makes me eager to savor their future flowering.

My beloved wife, Elana, is my partner as we continue to heed the lure toward greater love, greater engagement, greater joy. To have the blessing of sharing my life with my lifelong best friend is a true privilege and an abiding delight. She is an indefatigable advocate on behalf of our children and our family, and more than anyone I know makes her life a transparent reflection of God's best possibilities. In her the lure is alluring, and she is my inspiration.

To my beloved Elana I lovingly dedicate this book. Process Thinking teaches that we are never really separate, never truly apart. You are my breath.

Aharon aharon haviv—I am grateful beyond words to the Holy Blessing One. You create the world anew each moment, and you grace each and every one of us with the capacity to resonate to your invitation to love justice, renew covenant, and live a resilient life. As close as our respiration and as lustrous as the galaxies, you urge us to transcend our fears and to reach for our best possibilities. You are Shalom.

My blessing for us all is that we open ourselves to affirm God's invitation to manifest our optimum, to live most fully, and to relate most deeply, so that we co-evolve a world in which there is no more isolation, no more outcasts, and so that God—through us—can truly wipe away all tears, sighs, and sorrows. Then we, and God, will witness the *ge'ulah*/redemption that God and we have made actual.

Tam Venishlam Shevach Le-El Borei Olam.

Notes

Introduction

1. Literally "tree of life" (cf. Genesis 3:24, Proverbs 3:18), a favorite rabbinic metaphor for Torah in the broadest sense, the entirety of God and Jewry's ongoing revelation.

2. Bradley Shavit Artson, "Barukh Ha-Shem: God Is Bountiful," *Conservative Judaism*, Winter 1994, 32–43.

Chapter 1

1. As a religious Jew, while I revere the great medieval theologians—Rav Saadia and Rambam preeminent among them—I reserve the term *classical* for Torah: *Tanakh* (the Hebrew Bible) and Rabbinics (Mishnah, Talmud, Midrash, codes). I think that the medieval sages would have concurred with that prioritization. I acknowledge the influence and domination (but not the normative privilege or superiority) of the neo-platonizing Aristotelian scholastic blend, the so-called "classical" philosophical theology—Jewish, Christian, and Muslim—as "dominant."

2. For a superb presentation of Aristotelian premises and logic in the context of religious philosophy, there is no better presentation than Norbert M. Samuelson, *Revelation and the God of Israel* (Cambridge, UK: Cambridge University Press, 2002), pp. 22–28.

3. Job, by the way, provides brilliant evidence that such a response is not the only biblical ideal. His theologian friends work to get him to see the logic of accepting the blame in order to preserve God's omnipotence and omnibenevolence, yet Job refuses. God's response is to applaud Job's integrity and vision and to chastise Eliphaz and the other friends: "I am incensed at you and your two friends, for you have not spoken the truth about Me as did My servant Job" (Job 42:7).

4. See Hans Jonas, "The Concept of God after Auschwitz," in Lawrence Vogel, ed., *Mortality and Morality: A Search for the Good after Auschwitz* (Evanston, IL: Northwestern University Press, 1996), pp. 138–139; C. Robert Mesle, *Process Theology: A Basic Introduction* (St. Louis: Chalice Press, 1993), pp. 26–32; and John B. Cobb Jr., and David Ray Griffin, *Process Theology: An Introductory Exposition* (Louisville: Westminster John Knox Press, 1976), pp. 52–54.

5. See "El Shaddai" in Nahum M. Sarna, ed., *The JPS Commentary: Genesis* (Philadelphia: Jewish Publication Society, 1989), pp. 384–385.

6. Jonas, "Concept of God," p. 137.

7. Harold Kushner, "Would an All-Powerful God Be Worthy of Worship?" in Sandra B. Lubarsky and David Ray Griffin, eds., *Jewish Theology and Process Thought* (Albany: State University of New York Press, 1996), p. 90.

Chapter 2

1. This dynamism and relatedness is magnificently recounted in three books: Joel R. Primack and Nancy Ellen Abrams, *The View from the Center of the Universe: Discovering Our Extraordinary Place in the Cosmos* (New York: Riverhead Books, 2006); Brian Swimme and Thomas Berry, *The Universe Story: From the Primordial Flaring Forth to the Ecozoic Era—A Celebration of the Unfolding of the Cosmos* (New York: HarperOne, 1994); and Harold Morowitz, *The Emergence of Everything: How the World Became Complex* (New York: Oxford University Press, 2004).

2. Alfred North Whitehead called this *occasions of experience*. See Alfred North Whitehead, *Process and Reality*, corrected ed., ed. David Ray Griffin and Donald W. Sherburne (New York: The Free Press, 1978), p. 16; and David Ray Griffin, *Reenchantment without Supernaturalism: A Process Philosophy of Religion* (Ithaca, NY: Cornell University Press, 2001), pp. 108–109.

3. Whitehead's word for this immediate, internal intuition is *prehension*—that we immediately prehend all of existence. See John B. Cobb Jr., and David Ray Griffin, *Process Theology: An Introductory Exposition* (Louisville: Westminster John Knox Press, 1976), pp. 19–20.

4. Whitehead called this the *primordial aspect of God*, that part of God that is eternally fixed; the part of God that is unchanging because it has already been decided. See Jay McDaniel and Donna Bowman, eds., *Handbook of Process Theology* (St. Louis: Chalice Press, 2006), pp. 7–8.

5. McDaniel and Bowman, *Handbook*, p. 6.

6. Yehudah bar Ilai, Menahot 29b.

7. Rambam, *Mishneh Torah*, Hilkhot Teshuvah 5:1.

8. Rabbi Abraham ibn Ezra to Leviticus 22:31.

9. Most originally, Charles Hartshorne. See Charles Hartshorne and William L. Reese, *Philosophers Speak of God* (Amherst, NY: Humanity Books, 2000), pp. 1–15. Jeremiah 23:23–24. All biblical translations are taken from *Hebrew-English Tanakh: The Traditional Hebrew Text and the New JPS Translation*, ed. David E. S. Stein (Philadelphia: Jewish Publication Society, 1999).

10. Midrash Temurah, ch. 1.

11. Rabbi Yehudah Loew of Prague, *Chiddushei Aggadot* 2:89.

12. Rabbi Menahem Nahum of Chernobyl, *Me'or Einayim*, Chayei Sarah.

13. See Charles Hartshorne, "Some Causes of My Intellectual Growth," in Lewis Edwin Hahn, ed., *The Philosophy of Charles Hartshorne* (La Salle, IL: Open Court, 1991), p. 43.

14. Rabbi Moshe Cordovero, *Shiur Komah* to Zohar 3:14b (s.v. *idra rabba*).

Chapter 3

1. Tanhuma, Mishpatim 1, citing Psalm 99:4.

2. See Catherine Keller, "After Omnipotence: Power as Process," in *On the Mystery: Discerning God in Process* (Minneapolis: Fortress Press, 2008), pp. 69–90.

3. McDaniel and Bowman, *Handbook*, p. 7; Griffin, *Reenchantment*, pp. 146–147, 150–151.

4. Jonas, "Concept of God," p. 141.

5. Pesikta Rabbati xxvi, ed. Buber, p. 166b.

Chapter 4

1. Saadia Gaon, *The Book of Beliefs and Opinions*, trans. Samuel Rosenblatt (New Haven, CT: Yale University Press, 1948), Treatise 1, Exordium, p. 38.

2. See Primack and Abrams, *View*, pp. 156–166. As they point out, from the limit of our cosmic horizon, at 10^{28} cm as a maximum to the Planck length at the smallest (10^{-25} cm), there are about sixty orders of magnitude. Our intuition works near the center, from 10^{-5} cm to 10^5 cm. At sizes much larger or smaller than these, our assumptions, intuition, and logic no longer hold. The same limits pertain to time frames vastly more quick or more slow than the middle range of our own. The Uroborus comes from Nancy Abrams and Joel Primack, *The New Universe and the Human Future* (New Haven, CT: Yale University Press, 2010) and is reproduced here with the authors' kind permission. See also Sheldon Glashow with Ben Bova, *Interactions: A Journey through the Mind of a Particle Physicist and the Matter of This World* (New York: Warner Books, 1988), ch. 14; and Martin Rees, *Just Six Numbers: The Deep Forces That Shape the Universe* (New York: Basic Books, 2000), p. 8.

3. For discussions of other biblical texts on creation, see Terence E. Fretheim, *God and World in the Old Testament: A Relational Theology of Creation* (Nashville: Abingdon Press, 2005).

4. See Catherine Keller, *Face of the Deep: A Theology of Becoming* (London & New York: Routledge, 2003).

5. Rav Abraham Isaac Kook, *Orot Ha-Kodesh*.

6. Genesis 1:12, 21, 24.

7. See, for instance, Genesis 1:24. Discussion is found in Robert K. Gnuse, *The Old Testament and Process Theology* (St. Louis: Chalice Press, 2000), pp. 103–107.

8. Genesis 1:4, 10, 12, 18, 21, and 25.

9. Gnuse, *The Old Testament and Process Theology*, p. 102.

10. Zohar 1:207a.

11. Reb Simhah Bunam of Przysucha, *Siah Sarfei Kodesh*, 2:17.

12. Rabbi Shneur Zalman of Liadi, *Tanya*, ch. 25.

13. Primack and Abrams, *View*, p. 190.

14. See Martin Rees, and Neil deGrasse Tyson and Donald Goldsmith, *Origins: Fourteen Billion Years of Cosmic Evolution* (New York: W.W. Norton & Company, 2004), pp. 98–107.

15. The translation is taken from Moses Maimonides, *The Guide of the Perplexed*, trans. Shlomo Pines (Chicago: University of Chicago Press, 1963), II:22, p. 320.

Chapter 5

1. Moses Maimonides, *Guide of the Perplexed*, trans. Shlomo Pines (Chicago: University of Chicago Press, 1963), III:12, p. 442.

2. NJPS translates this phrase as "I make weal and create woe."

3. Maimonides, *Guide of the Perplexed*, III:12, p. 443.

4. Ibid., p. 444.

5. Ibid., p. 445.

Chapter 6

1. Whitehead, *Religion in the Making* (New York: Fordham University Press, 1996), p. 144.

2. Keller, *On the Mystery*, pp. xii–xiii.

3. My translation, based on *Selected Religious Poems of Solomon ibn Gabirol*, ed. Israel Davidson (Philadelphia: Jewish Publication Society of America, 1924), p. 8.

4. Shneur Zalman, *Tanya* (New York: Kehot Publishing Company, 1996), ch. 42.

5. *A Treasury of Jewish Quotations*, ed. Joseph L. Baron (New York: Thomas Yoseloff LTD, 1965), p. 415.

6. Maimonides, *Guide of the Perplexed,* I:54 p. 123.

7. *Or Adonai,* Vienna ed., book 2, part 4, 41a.

8. Jakob Petuchowski, *Studies in Modern Theology and Prayer* (Philadelphia: Jewish Publication Society, 1998), p. 110.

9. Arthur A. Cohen, *The Natural and the Supernatural Jew* (New York: Free Press, 1988), p. 291.

10. For more examples, see Bradley Shavit Artson, "Halakhah and Ethics: The Holy and the Good," *Conservative Judaism,* Spring 1994, pp. 70–88; and Reuven Hammer, *The Torah Revolution: Fourteen Truths That Changed the World* (Woodstock, VT: Jewish Lights Publishing, 2011).

11. See Menachem Elon, *The Principles of Jewish Law* (Jerusalem: Keter Publishing House, 1974), p. 55.

Chapter 7

1. Maimonides, introduction to ch. 10 of Mishnah Sanhedrin.

2. Louis Jacobs, *A Jewish Theology* (New York: Behrman House, 1973), p. 321.

Chapter 8

1. Martin Buber, *Tales of the Hasidim: The Later Masters* (New York: Schocken Books, 1948), p. 86.

2. Catherine Keller, *On the Mystery* (Minneapolis: Fortress Press, 2008), pp. xii–xiii.

3. Letter to Edith Hahn, 16.1.1920.

4. Buber, *Tales of the Hasidim: The Later Masters,* p. 264.

Chapter 9

1. *Ebony,* August 1970, p. 115.

2. Maimonides, *Guide of the Perplexed,* III: 8, p. 431.

3. Ibid., pp. 431–432.

4. *The Nineteen Letters of Ben Uziel,* "Eleventh Letter," p. 112.

Chapter 10

1. Jonas, *Mortality and Morality,* p. 70.

2. Charlotte Fonrobert, "To Increase Torah Is to Increase Life," in *The Meaning of Life in the World Religions,* ed. Joseph Runzo and Nancy M. Martin (Oxford, UK: Oneworld, 2000), p. 88.

Chapter 11

1. John Cobb, "Process Theology," http://processandfaith.org/writings/article/process-theology (accessed May 20, 2013).

2. Ian G. Barbour, *When Science Meets Religion: Enemies, Strangers, or Partners?* (San Francisco: HarperSanFrancisco, 2000), p. 164.

3. Keller, *On the Mystery*, p. 52.

4. Keller, *On the Mystery*, p. 104.

5. "Process Theology" by John B. Cobb Jr.; http://www.religion-online.org/show-article.asp?title=1489 (accessed May 20, 2013).

Chapter 12

1. Y. Pe'ah 2:17a. See also Sifrei Deuteronomy 11:13 and Y. Megillah 1:7.

2. Hans Jonas, *Memoirs*, ed. Christian Wiese (Waltham, MA: Brandeis University Press, 2008), p. 30.

3. Rabbi Shneur Zalman of Liadi, *Tanya*, ch. 25.

4. Zohar 3: 234a.

5. Pesikta Rabbati, Piska 3.

6. See Joshua A. Berman, *Created Equal: How the Bible Broke with Ancient Political Thought* (New York and Oxford: Oxford University Press, 2008).

7. Sifrei Deuteronomy, Piska 312.

8. Pesikta Rabbati, Piska 21.

9. Tanhuma (Warsaw Edition), Ekev, ch. 3.

Chapter 13

1. Jonas, *Memoirs*, p. 118.

2. Leo Strauss, *Preface to Spinoza's Critique of Religion*, 20.

Chapter 14

1. Marjorie Hewitt Suchocki, *In God's Presence: Theological Reflections on Prayer* (St. Louis: Chalice Press, 1996), p. 18.

Chapter 15

1. Jonas, *Mortality and Morality*, p. 70.

Chapter 16

1. Alfred North Whitehead, *Process and Reality* (New York: Free Press, 1975), p. 29.

2. Alfred North Whitehead, "Immortality," in *Essays in Science and Philosophy* (New York: Greenwood Press, 1968), p. 94.

3. Pesikta Rabbati 12:1

Conclusion

1. Saadia Gaon, *Book of Beliefs and Opinions*, trans. Samuel Rosenblatt (New Haven, CT: Yale University Press, 1948) p. 158.

For Further Exploration
Process Resources

Select Bibliography

Cobb, John B., Jr. *Praying for Jennifer: An Exploration of Intercessory Prayer in Story Form.* Eugene, OR: Wipf and Stock Publishers, 1985.

———. *The Process Perspective: Frequently Asked Questions about Process Theology.* Edited by Jeanyne B. Slettom. St. Louis: Chalice Press, 2003.

———. *The Process Perspective II.* Edited by Jeanyne B. Slettom. St. Louis: Chalice Press, 2011.

Cobb, John B., Jr., and David Ray Griffin. *Process Theology: An Introductory Exposition.* Louisville: Westminster John Knox Press, 1976.

Griffin, David Ray. *Reenchantment without Supernaturalism: A Process Philosophy of Religion.* Ithaca, NY: Cornell University Press, 2001.

Keller, Catherine. *On the Mystery: Discerning God in Process.* Minneapolis: Fortress Press, 2008.

McDaniel, Jay, and Donna Bowman, eds. *Handbook of Process Theology.* St. Louis: Chalice Press, 2006.

Mesle, C. Robert. *Process-Relational Philosophy: An Introduction to Alfred North Whitehead.* West Conshohocken, PA: Templeton Press, 2008.

———. *Process Theology: A Basic Introduction.* St. Louis: Chalice Press, 1993.

Rescher, Nicholas. *Process Philosophy: A Survey of Basic Issues.* Pittsburgh: University of Pittsburgh Press, 2000.

Suchocki, Marjorie Hewitt. *In God's Presence: Theological Reflections on Prayer.* St. Louis: Chalice Press, 1996.

Other Resources

Center for Process Studies
1325 N. College Avenue
Claremont, CA 91711
www.ctr4process.org

Jesus, Jazz, Buddhism
www.jesusjazzbuddhism.org/index.html

Process & Faith
www.processandfaith.org

Ziegler School of Rabbinic Studies Process Theology Podcasts
www.zieglertorah.org/category/process/

A theology that helps us appreciate Judaism for what it was intended to be—and truly is.

"Process Thought's relational way of describing the cosmos and the Divine, the nature of becoming and of reality, changes our understanding of creation, revelation, commandments, ethics, prayer, Israel, death, freedom and love. Accordingly, this book offers a two-tiered opportunity to grow in this new understanding."

—FROM THE INTRODUCTION

Process Thought is a systematic approach for integrating religion and science in a way that respects the integrity of both disciplines as valid ways to relate to each other and the world. This examination of Process Thought from a Jewish perspective applies key Process insights to major aspects of Judaism to show how this powerful theological tool can unlock the true impact and resonance of Jewish sources and wisdom.

In an accessible and inviting way, it introduces Process Thought's major themes of dynamic, interconnected and continuous relational change by exploring Judaism's:

- • Relationship with God and Israel
- Commitment to covenant
- Rituals and observances, including prayer, *mitzvot* and holy days
- Understanding of mortality and meaning
- Connection to community and the pursuit of justice

"Crisply written, this volume offers delicious food for thought and will be accessible to followers of various religions."

—American Library Association's *Booklist*

Also by Rabbi Bradley Shavit Artson, DHL

Renewing the Process of Creation
A Jewish Integration of Science and Spirit

A daring blend of Jewish theology, science and Process Thought, exploring personal actions through Judaism and the sciences as dynamically interactive and mutually informative.

6 x 9, 208 pp, HC, 978-1-58023-833-5

Passing Life's Tests
Spiritual Reflections on the Trial of Abraham, the Binding of Isaac

Presents this powerful tale as a tool for our own soul wrestling, to transcend its words to confront our own existential sacrifices and our ability to face—and surmount—life's tests.

6 x 9, 176 pp, Quality PB, 978-1-58023-631-7

Rabbi Bradley Shavit Artson, DHL, an inspiring speaker and educator, holds the Abner and Roslyn Goldstine Dean's Chair of the Ziegler School of Rabbinic Studies and is vice president of American Jewish University in Los Angeles. He is a member of the philosophy department, supervises the Miller Introduction to Judaism Program and mentors Camp Ramah in California and in Monterey Bay. He is also dean of Zacharias Frankel College in Potsdam, Germany, ordaining rabbis for Europe. A regular columnist for the *Huffington Post*, he is author of many articles and books, including *Renewing the Process of Creation: A Jewish Integration of Science and Spirit* and *Passing Life's Tests: Spiritual Reflections on the Trial of Abraham, the Binding of Isaac.*

"The most comprehensive exposition of a Jewish Process Theology yet written. Jews and Gentiles alike are indebted to Rabbi Artson for the intellectual-theological-emotional achievement this book represents."

—**Rabbi David Ellenson**, president,
Hebrew Union College–Jewish Institute of Religion

Also Available

Our Religious Brains
What Cognitive Science Reveals about Belief, Morality, Community and Our Relationship with God
By Rabbi Ralph D. Mecklenburger
Foreword by Dr. Howard Kelfer; Preface by Dr. Neil Gillman
A groundbreaking, accessible look at the implications of cognitive science for religion and theology.
6 x 9, 224 pp, HC, 978-1-58023-508-2
Quality PB, 978-1-58023-840-3

Jewish Theology in Our Time
A New Generation Explores the Foundations & Future of Jewish Belief
Edited by Rabbi Elliot J. Cosgrove, PhD
Foreword by Rabbi David J. Wolpe
Preface by Rabbi Carole B. Balin, PhD
Brings together a cross section of interesting new voices from all movements in Judaism to inspire and stimulate discussion now and in the years to come.
6 x 9, 240 pp, HC, 978-1-58023-413-9
Quality PB, 978-1-58023-630-0

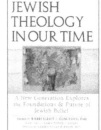

God & the Big Bang, 2nd Ed.
Discovering Harmony between Science & Spirituality
By Daniel C. Matt
This update of the award-winning first edition draws on both science and theology, fact and belief, cosmology and Jewish mysticism, to discover the presence of God throughout the cosmos and in our everyday lives.
6 x 9, 224 pp, Quality PB, 978-1-58023-836-6

For People of All Faiths, All Backgrounds
JEWISH LIGHTS Publishing

An imprint of Turner Publishing Company
Nashville, Tennessee
Tel: (615) 255-2665   Fax: (615) 255-5081

www.jewishlights.com
www.turnerpublishing.com
Find us on Facebook®
Facebook is a registered trademark of Facebook, Inc.